Always in Season

A Collection of Recipes from
the Junior League of Salt Lake City, Utah

The George S. & Dolores Doré Eccles Foundation

proudly supports the

Junior League of Salt Lake City

for its commitment and dedication

to improving the lives of

women and children in our community.

Always in Season

A Collection of Recipes from
the Junior League of Salt Lake City, Utah

Published by the
Junior League of Salt Lake
City, Inc.

Copyright 1999 by the
Junior League of Salt Lake
City, Inc.

Junior League of Salt Lake City
438 East 200 South, Suite 200
Salt Lake City, Utah 84111
801-328-1019

Library of Congress Number:
98-066594
ISBN: 0-9616972-2-9

Edited, Designed and
Manufactured by
Favorite Recipes Press
an imprint of

FRP

P.O. Box 305142
Nashville, Tennessee 37230
1-800-358-0560

Book Design: David Malone
Art Director: Steve Newman
Project Manager: Jane Hinshaw

Manufactured in
the United States of America

First Printing:
1999 30,000 copies

Credits

Food Photographer

Brent Herridge has been a commercial photographer for over
25 years. He studied photography at the University of Utah and
later became an instructor in that program for five years. Currently
Brent owns and manages a marketing and communications
company specializing in shopping center and retail advertising
across the nation. His artistic talent and creative eye for visual
images are emphasized in the work his agency produces.
His work has now been featured in two cookbooks published
by the Junior League of Salt Lake City.

Scenic Photographer

Tom Till is one of the West's most published photographers.
He resides in Moab with wife Marci and children Bryce, Mikenna,
and Christina. Several of his Utah photographic collections
are best-sellers, including *Utah, A Celebration of the Landscape*
(Westcliffe Publishers). The Tom Till Gallery, at 61 North Main
in Moab, features prints, books, and other products by Tom.
Call 1-888-479-9808 for a free catalog.

Food Stylist

Susan Massey has been a professional food stylist in San
Francisco for 17 years. Her work includes numerous cookbooks,
print features, and television commercials. A Salt Lake City
resident from 1970 to 1977, she moved back to Utah in 1994 to be
close to her daughter and grandson. She now commutes between
Salt Lake City and San Francisco on a regular basis.

Writer

Virginia Rainey was born and raised in Salt Lake City. After college
she moved to San Francisco, where she worked and learned about
food for 20 years. During that time she co-authored *California the
Beautiful* cookbook. She returned to Utah in 1994 and is a freelance
marketing communications writer as well as a food and wine
feature writer for various print and on-line publications.

Contents

The crossed knife-and-fork symbol marks recipes that are featured on menus.

The chef's hat symbol marks recipes that have been contributed by chefs and restaurants.

The Junior League of Salt Lake City, Inc.

The Junior League of Salt Lake City, Inc., is an organization of women committed to promoting voluntarism and to improving the community through the effective action and leadership of trained volunteers. Its purpose is exclusively educational and charitable.

The Junior League of Salt Lake City anticipates needs and creates positive change for all women and children through collaborative programs and effective advocacy by providing resources and leadership for our community.

Serving the community since 1931, the following projects have benefited the Salt Lake community:

AIDS Education	Law Related Education
Art of the Challenged	Lollapalooza
Art Start	Museum of Natural History
Boardwalk	Neighborhood House
C.A.R.E. Fair	Omnibus
Child Care Connection	Pine Canyon Boys Ranch
Children's Justice Center	Rape Crisis Center
Community Training Center	Ready or Not
Consumer Health Information Center	Ronald McDonald House
Court Resources	S.O.S. (Seniors on Stage)
Family Support Center	Salt Lake Art Center
Here to Help	Sharing Place
Hogle Zoo	SMILES
Hospice	STAR
Junior Achievement	Utah Children's Center
Junior Science Academy	Utah Opera Company
Juvenile Court	Utah Youth Village
Kidspace	You're in Charge
KUED	Wheeler Farm
KUER	Women Helping Women

55+ Senior Resource Directory

Introduction

With a bounty of foods and scenic photographs that reveal the subtle and dramatic changes the seasons bring, this book celebrates the stunning diversity and beauty of Utah's land and waters. Only in Utah will you encounter the contrast of 12,000-foot alpine peaks with river-sliced canyons that reveal all 13 periods of the geologic time scale. In between, we have the best of all worlds, including rivers, lakes, and thriving cities with easy access to canyons, forests, wilderness, and national parks. Residents know that along with family, friends, and the seasons, the geography is what keeps us here, and that the memory and dramatic feeling of the landscape is what draws people back to the state after years spent elsewhere, just as it entices and captures people from the world over.

Because of that, the recipes collected here are as diverse as our landscape. But whatever the category, when a recipe includes herbs, fruits, or vegetables, we emphasize the importance of using fresh ingredients for ultimate flavor—and to capture the essence of the season. Along with a variety of recipes, food tips, and tidbits about Utah, each chapter of *Always in Season* features two menus, wine suggestions, and an invaluable section on can't-live-without "Seasonal Essentials." All in all, we hope this book will help you discover that good cooking is *Always in Season* in Utah.

Through spring, summer, autumn, and winter in Utah, Always in Season *celebrates the joys of cooking and sharing food with family and friends.*

Some of our recipes are quick and easy and some are elaborate. We've included light and healthy recipes as well as the occasional indulgence. Down-home comfort foods, chef's specialties from some of our favorite restaurants, international classics, and local color— it's all here.

Spring

Spring dresses Utah's Antelope Island in a gorgeous gown of blooms—including white evening primrose and brilliant red and yellow claret cup. This is where, in the southern reaches of the Great Salt Lake, antelope, coyote, and buffalo roam just miles from the booming Wasatch Front. It's also a great destination for bird-watching.

In many areas of Utah, spring arrives with the unmistakable scents of apricot, apple, and cherry blossoms wafting through the air. And it seems that everywhere below about 5,000 feet the landscape is punctuated with thousands of crocus, tulips, and daffodils. Around Temple Square in downtown Salt Lake, the beautiful Easter-basket-colored gardens are a sight to behold. As for outdoor fun, spring brings something for everyone—from snow for fair-weather skiers to sunny days for mountain bikers, fishermen, and, of course, gardeners.

In the markets, most spring produce still arrives from out of state. But that doesn't stop cooks from stocking up on all the traditional ingredients that symbolize the fertile season, including asparagus and new potatoes, fresh spring peas, lamb, and ham. Herbs, such as rosemary and mint, add to the fresh feeling of the new season. If the days are warm enough, there will be some sweet cherries and the crops of local raspberries by June.

Flavored Butters

It's always good to have some flavored butter on hand to toss with fresh spring vegetables or to place on top of grilled broiled steaks, chops, poultry, and fish just before serving. Always start with the real thing—fresh unsalted butter—and make it when you have the ingredients available so it will be ready to spread at a moment's notice. The easiest butter of all is Herb Butter, *which is made by simply combining 1 tablespoon of freshly chopped herb of your choice with 4 ounces of softened butter.*

Maitre d'Hotel Butter

$^1\!/_2$ cup unsalted butter, softened
1 tablespoon freshly squeezed lemon juice
2 to 3 tablespoons finely minced shallot or scallion
salt and freshly ground pepper to taste

Beat the butter in a mixer bowl until light and fluffy. Add the lemon juice, shallot, salt and pepper and mix well. Spoon into a serving container and cover, or roll into a log and wrap in plastic wrap. Chill until serving time. Freeze for later use if desired.

Raspberry Basil Butter

$^1\!/_2$ cup unsalted butter, softened
$^1\!/_3$ cup fresh or thawed frozen raspberries
1 tablespoon raspberry jam
1 tablespoon red wine
4 large basil leaves, chopped

Combine the butter, raspberries, jam, wine and basil in a bowl and mix well. Chill until serving time. Serve on crusty French bread, biscuits, scones, fruit muffins, pancakes and waffles.

Spring Essentials

Spring Essentials

Artichokes

Although artichokes are available year-round, they are at their best in the late spring. Enjoy them cold or hot with a variety of dipping sauces. Choose firm, dark green artichokes with tightly closed leaves. To prepare them for cooking, rinse in cool water and cut the stems almost flush with the base. Trim the spiky point off the outside leaves with kitchen scissors.

Combine the whole artichoke with a pinch of salt, a squeeze of fresh lemon juice and water to cover in a deep stockpot. Cook for 40 minutes or until the bottom of the choke can be easily pierced with a fork, adding water as needed to cover. Lift the artichoke from the water with long tongs to test for doneness; drain.

Serve the whole artichoke with a butter or sauce for dipping; guests can peel away the leaves, dip them into the sauce and pull the artichoke meat off the ends of the leaves with their teeth.

Use a grapefruit spoon or sharp knife to cut away the thin leaves and the fibrous center portion to expose the tender artichoke heart when the outer leaves are gone.

For Lemon Butter to serve with artichokes, combine the juice of 2 lemons, 1/2 cup melted butter, 2 tablespoons chopped fresh parsley and freshly ground pepper to taste.

For Herb Mayonnaise, combine 1 cup mayonnaise, 1/4 cup lemon juice and 1/4 cup chopped dill.

To stuff artichokes or to serve them in a formal setting, remove the fibrous centers before serving. Use the heel of the hand to strike the artichoke sharply on the top. Gently remove the center leaves and use a spoon to remove the fibrous part, leaving the heart and bottom intact. You can also cool the artichoke completely, cut it into quarters, and scoop out the fibrous center easily.

"The artichoke is the only vegetable that, when you finish eating it, you have more on your plate than when you started." Anonymous

Tossed Green Salad with a Basic Vinaigrette Dressing

Spring is the season to enjoy fresh salads. The quality of a salad rests on the quality of each ingredient. Basically, you should find the freshest, most crisp greens you can and coat them lightly with vinaigrette made with extra-virgin olive oil or salad oil. Vary your vinegars and oils according to taste: walnut oil and sherry vinegar make a delicious combination for a change. You can buy a mix of baby greens, generally sold as "mesclun" or "salad greens," or put your own mix together.

1 tablespoon wine vinegar
$^1/_4$ teaspoon salt
$^1/_8$ teaspoon freshly ground pepper
$^1/_2$ cup extra-virgin olive oil or salad oil
4 cups mixed greens or mesclun

Mix the vinegar and salt in a small bowl, stirring to dissolve the salt. Add the pepper. Whisk in the oil. Store in a jar in the refrigerator until serving time.

Rinse the salad greens and dry in a spinner or blot dry with paper towels. Tear larger leaves into bite-size pieces and combine all greens in a salad bowl. Shake or stir the vinaigrette. Pour evenly over the greens and toss to coat.

For Vinaigrette with Fresh Herbs, add 1 teaspoon chopped fresh herbs such as tarragon, chervil or parsley.

For Mustard Vinaigrette, add $1^1/_2$ teaspoons Dijon mustard or whole-grain mustard with the pepper.

For Bleu Cheese Vinaigrette, add $1^1/_2$ tablespoons bleu cheese.

For Fruit Salad Vinaigrette, use lemon juice instead of vinegar and add $^1/_3$ cup honey and an optional teaspoon of poppy seeds.

Spring Essentials

Spring Essentials

Marinade for Pork, Lamb or Chicken

Marinades tenderize, moisten, and flavor meats and vegetables. The variations are endless but are usually based on a combination of an acid—such as vinegar, wine, fruit juice, or yogurt—an oil, and a flavoring. To use the marinade for basting, set some aside before adding the meat. Otherwise the marinade should be boiled for at least 5 minutes before using in order to avoid bacteria from the uncooked meat; discard any unused marinade that has been in contact with the meat.

1/2 cup vegetable oil
1/4 cup olive oil
juice and zest of 2 lemons
1 small onion, minced
1 teaspoon salt
1 teaspoon freshly ground pepper
1 cup mixed herbs

Whisk the vegetable oil, olive oil, lemon juice, lemon zest, onion, salt and pepper in a shallow glass dish.

Add rosemary and thyme for pork, chicken or lamb; add mint and tarragon for chicken. Whisk to mix well.

Reserve any marinade that will be used for basting. Add the meat of choice to the remaining marinade. Marinate, covered, in the refrigerator according to the recipe chosen.

Grill, roast, broil or bake the meat, basting with the reserved marinade.

When marinating any food, be sure that it is completely covered with the marinade. Use a glass or ceramic container, and marinate, covered, in the refrigerator until 30 minutes before grilling, as meat will cook more quickly and evenly if it is not chilled. The length of time required for marinating depends on the type of food. Larger cuts of meat, tougher cuts of meat (such as flank steak), and bone-in chicken should be marinated for 8 hours or longer. Fish and boneless chicken should marinate for a short time.

A Family Gathering

Grilled Pork Tenderloin with Spice Rub
Pineapple Mango Salsa
Color Country Vegetables
Fresh Peas with Lemon Zest
Baby New Potatoes
Lemon Chess Tart with Whipped Cream
Springtime Tea
Champagne and Orange Mimosas

Spring Fever

Spinach and Feta Spirals
Citrus Salad Toss
Lamb Burgers with Yogurt Dill Sauce
Log Haven Carrot Risotto
Whipping Cream Cake with Fresh Berries
Jumbo Chocolate Chip Cookies
Iced Herbal Tea
Red Rock Brewing Bavarian Weiss

Menus

Spring Menus

Chef Marguerite Henderson notes, "This is a wonderful introduction to the joy of scraping the 'meat' off the artichoke leaves for children. They love the bread crumb stuffing, as do adults. My mother would make these for traditional Sunday dinners in our Italian home in Brooklyn."

Stuffed Artichokes alla Siciliana

Ingredients
3 tablespoons butter
3 tablespoons olive oil
2 large cloves of garlic, minced
2 cups fresh bread crumbs
1 teaspoon dried oregano
1 teaspoon dried basil
salt to taste
¼ teaspoon pepper
¼ cup grated Romano cheese
¼ cup chopped fresh parsley
6 fresh artichokes
2 lemons, cut into halves

Garnish
lemon slices

Heat the butter and olive oil in a medium skillet over medium heat. Add the garlic and sauté for 1 minute or until fragrant. Add the bread crumbs, oregano, basil, salt and pepper. Cook for 2 minutes or until lightly toasted, tossing to cook evenly. Remove from the heat and add the cheese and parsley; toss lightly.

Trim the edges of the artichokes with scissors. Slice off the bottoms to stand upright. Place each trimmed artichoke in a large bowl of water with 1 lemon until all are trimmed to prevent browning. Drain the artichokes and strike upside down on the counter to spread the leaves. Remove the purple spiny choke from the center of each with a sharp knife.

Place a small amount of the stuffing into each leaf with a teaspoon. Place the stuffed artichokes upright in a deep saucepan that will hold them tightly. Add 2 inches of water. Add the remaining lemon. Cook, covered, over medium heat for 50 to 60 minutes or until tender, checking every 15 minutes and adding water as needed.

Garnish with lemon slices and serve as a first course with lots of crusty bread.

Serves Six

Spring

Utah's spring "Green Globe" artichokes, which are the most plentiful, have a deeper, more nutty flavor than those found in the market in the middle of winter. Artichokes will look and taste fresh for up to two weeks if handled properly. Do not wash before storing. To keep longer than a few days, just drizzle a few drops of water on each artichoke, place it in a plastic bag, seal the bag airtight, and refrigerate in the coldest part of the refrigerator.

To prepare a fresh pineapple, twist off the crown and slice the pineapple into quarters lengthwise. Slide the knife along the shell to remove the fruit and slice away the hard core.

Pineapple Mango Salsa

Peel and finely chop the mango. Combine with the pineapple, onion, celery, bell pepper and green chiles in a bowl. Add the cilantro and lime juice and mix well. Serve with corn chips or as an accompaniment to grilled fish.

Substitute 2 chopped and seeded Anaheim peppers for the green chiles if desired.

Serves Six

Ingredients

1 mango
3 cups finely chopped fresh
   pineapple
$1/2$ cup chopped red onion
1 cup chopped celery
$1/4$ cup chopped red bell
   pepper
1 (4-ounce) can chopped
   green chiles
$1/4$ cup chopped fresh
   cilantro
$1/4$ cup lime juice

Spinach and Feta Spirals

Sauté the green onions in the heated olive oil in a medium skillet over medium heat for 1 minute. Remove to a large bowl and cool. Stir in the spinach, feta cheese, lemon juice, nutmeg, salt and pepper. Add the egg yolk and mix well.

Thaw the puff pastry. Roll to a 13x13-inch square on a floured surface. Cut lengthwise into two 6$1/2$x13-inch strips. Spread the spinach filling evenly over the strips, leaving a 1-inch border on all sides. Brush the edges with milk. Roll each strip from the long side to enclose the filling; press the edges firmly to seal. Place on a buttered baking sheet.

Cut 1-inch slashes in the tops of the rolls at $3/4$-inch intervals. Brush with milk. Bake at 400 degrees for 25 minutes or until golden brown. Cool slightly. Remove to a cutting board. Cut into slices on the slash marks. Serve warm.

Makes Three Dozen

Ingredients

$3/4$ cup sliced green onions
1 tablespoon olive oil
1 (10-ounce) package
   frozen chopped spinach,
   thawed, squeezed dry
$1^1/2$ cups crumbled feta
   cheese
1 tablespoon lemon juice
$1/4$ teaspoon nutmeg
salt and pepper to taste
1 large egg yolk
1 sheet frozen puff pastry
milk

Serve Elegant Swedish Shrimp on a clear glass plate and let the onions, capers, and bay leaves in the recipe serve as the garnish.

Elegant Swedish Shrimp

For the marinade, combine the oil, vinegar, undrained capers, Tabasco sauce, celery seeds and salt in a bowl; mix well.

For the shrimp, combine the celery tops, pickling spices and salt with a large saucepan of water and bring to a boil. Add the shrimp and reduce the heat. Simmer, covered for 5 minutes; drain. Peel and devein the shrimp under cold water.

Layer the shrimp, onion rings and bay leaves in a shallow dish. Pour the marinade over the layers. Marinate, covered, for 24 hours or longer, basting occasionally. Serve with wooden picks.

Serves Eight

Caper Marinade
1¼ cups salad oil
¾ cup white vinegar
3 tablespoons capers with
    juice
dash of Tabasco sauce
2½ teaspoons celery seeds
1½ teaspoons salt

Shrimp
½ cup chopped celery tops
¼ cup mixed pickling
    spices
3½ teaspoons salt
2 to 2½ pounds fresh or
    frozen shrimp in shells
2 cups sliced onions, in
    rings or halved rings
8 bay leaves

Parmesan Stars

Combine the Parmesan cheese, onion, mayonnaise and pepper in a bowl and mix well. Chill in the refrigerator for 8 hours or longer.

Cut each slice of bread with a star cutter. Spread about 2 tablespoons of the cheese mixture evenly on each star. Arrange on a large baking sheet. Bake at 400 degrees for 5 to 7 minutes or until bubbly and golden brown. Serve immediately.

Serves Twenty-Four

Ingredients
¾ cup grated Parmesan
    cheese
¼ cup finely grated onion
½ cup mayonnaise
¼ teaspoon pepper
24 slices white bread

Cream of Asparagus Soup

Cook half the asparagus in ¼ of the chicken broth in a saucepan just until tender-crisp. Remove from the heat and reserve.

Sauté the onion and celery in the butter in a skillet until tender. Cook the remaining asparagus in enough water to cover the asparagus in a saucepan until tender; drain. Combine with the sautéed mixture in a blender container and process until puréed.

Combine the puréed mixture with the remaining chicken broth in a saucepan and mix well. Cook until heated through. Stir in the whipping cream and half-and-half. Cook just until heated through. Stir in the reserved asparagus.

Serve hot or cold. Garnish with mint.

Serves Six to Eight

Ingredients
2 bunches asparagus, cut
   into small pieces
1 (14-ounce) can chicken
   broth
1 small onion, chopped
1 rib celery, chopped
2 tablespoons butter
½ pint whipping cream
1 pint half-and-half

Garnish
mint sprigs

Carrot Ginger Soup

Ingredients
1 onion, thinly sliced
2 cloves of garlic, minced
3 tablespoons butter
2 pounds carrots, peeled,
    chopped
1 tablespoon grated fresh
    ginger
6 cups vegetable stock
1 teaspoon salt
1 teaspoon white pepper
1 cup half-and-half
    (optional)

Sauté the onion and garlic in the butter in a saucepan until translucent. Add the carrots and ginger and sauté for several minutes.

Add the vegetable stock, salt and white pepper. Simmer, covered, until the carrots are very tender.

Purée in a food processor or with an immersion blender until smooth and creamy, adjusting the consistency with additional vegetable stock or half-and-half if necessary. Add the half-and-half and cook just until heated through.

Ladle into warmed soup bowls and garnish with chives or croutons.

This soup may be served chilled instead of hot, or you may omit the ginger and add fresh dill or other herbs of your choice.

Serves Six

Spring

Use portobello mushrooms in Promontory Point Tortellini Soup for a richer flavor. This recipe can be easily doubled.

Promontory Point Tortellini Soup

Heat the olive oil in a large heavy saucepan over medium heat. Add the mushrooms and garlic. Sauté for 5 minutes or until tender. Add the chicken broth and bring to a boil.

Add the tortellini. Cook, loosely covered, for 5 minutes or until the tortellini are al dente. Add the spinach. Simmer for 2 minutes or until the spinach is wilted. Stir in the Parmesan cheese, salt and pepper.

Ladle the soup into bowls and serve with additional grated Parmesan cheese.

Serves Two

Ingredients
2 tablespoons olive oil
4 ounces mushrooms, thinly sliced
2 large cloves of garlic, chopped
3 (14-ounce) cans reduced-sodium chicken broth
1 (9-ounce) package chicken tortellini
3 cups thinly sliced spinach leaves
2 tablespoons grated Parmesan cheese
salt and pepper to taste

The first transcontinental railroad was completed at Promontory, Utah, in May of 1869. The Golden Spike National Historic Site, about 32 miles west of Brigham City, marks the spot. The railroads changed the way America ate as, suddenly, it was easy to get fresh produce from California or to send crops out to the nation.

Substitute one package Mediterranean or European prepared salad mix for the leaf lettuce and butter lettuce in this recipe if you prefer.

Artichoke and Mandarin Orange Salad

Basic Vinaigrette
1/4 teaspoon paprika
1/2 teaspoon dry mustard
1/4 teaspoon sugar
2 teaspoons water
1/2 cup red wine or
    balsamic vinegar
1/2 cup olive oil
2 cloves of garlic, sliced

Salad
1 head red leaf lettuce
1 head Boston or Bibb
    lettuce
1 (11-ounce) can mandarin
    oranges, drained
1 (6-ounce) jar marinated
    artichoke hearts, drained
salt and freshly ground
    pepper to taste
1/2 cup crumbled bleu
    cheese

For the vinaigrette, mix the paprika, dry mustard and sugar in a small bowl. Whisk in the water and vinegar. Drizzle in the olive oil gradually, whisking constantly. Add the garlic. Chill until serving time.

For the salad, tear the leaf lettuce and Boston lettuce into small pieces. Combine with the mandarin oranges and artichoke hearts in a bowl. Season with salt and pepper.

Remove and discard the garlic slices from the vinaigrette. Pour the vinaigrette over the salad at serving time. Add the bleu cheese and toss lightly to mix well.

Serves Six to Eight

Treat yourself to a zester to remove just the tangy outer peel of citrus and leave the white pith. It has a short metal blade with five tiny holes that will remove thin strips of peel for everything from salads to steamed vegetables or desserts.

Citrus Salad Toss

For the pecans, mix the sugar with the pecans in a small skillet. Cook over low heat until the sugar melts, stirring to coat the pecans well. Spread on foil and cool; break pecans apart.

For the dressing, combine the oil, lime juice, orange juice, sugar, lime zest and orange zest in an airtight jar and shake well. Chill until serving time.

For the salad, combine the lettuce, onion, oranges and strawberries in a large salad bowl and toss gently. Chill until serving time.

Add the avocados to the salad just before serving. Drizzle with the dressing and toss gently. Top with the pecans.

Mandarin oranges may be substituted for the fresh orange.

Serves Four to Six

Sugared Pecans
1/4 cup sugar
2/3 cup pecan halves

Citrus Dressing
2/3 cup vegetable oil
1/4 cup lime juice
2 tablespoons orange juice
2 tablespoons sugar
1 teaspoon grated lime zest
1 teaspoon grated orange zest

Salad
8 cups torn leaf lettuce
8 cups torn Romaine lettuce
1 red onion, thinly sliced
1 large orange, peeled, sliced
1 pint strawberries, cut into halves
2 avocados, thinly sliced

Spinach and Apple Salad with Bacon

Mustard Vinaigrette
1/4 cup vegetable oil
3 tablespoons red wine
 vinegar
1 teaspoon sugar
1/2 teaspoon prepared
 mustard
salt and pepper to taste

Salad
5 slices bacon
1/4 cup sliced almonds
8 cups torn fresh spinach
1 unpeeled red apple,
 chopped
3 green onions, sliced

For the vinaigrette, combine the oil, vinegar, sugar, mustard, salt and pepper in a covered jar; shake to blend well. Store in the refrigerator for up to 2 days.

For the salad, cook the bacon in a skillet until crisp. Remove, drain and crumble the bacon, reserving 1 tablespoon drippings in the skillet.

Add the almonds to the skillet. Cook over high heat until the almonds are browned, shaking constantly.

Combine the spinach, apple and green onions in a large salad bowl. Add the bacon and almonds. Add the vinaigrette and toss to mix well.

Serves Six

Red Potato Salad

Place the potatoes in a saucepan and cover with water. Cook for 15 minutes or until tender; drain. Cool the potatoes and cut into halves.

Combine the potatoes, eggs, carrot and scallions in a large bowl. Add the dill, parsley, caraway seeds, salt and pepper; toss to mix well.

Combine the sour cream and mayonnaise in a bowl and mix well. Fold into the potato mixture. Chill for several hours before serving.

Serves Eight

Ingredients
14 small red new potatoes with skins
6 hard-cooked eggs, cut into halves
1 carrot, peeled, grated
2 scallions, thinly sliced
3 tablespoons chopped fresh dill
2 tablespoons chopped fresh parsley
1 tablespoon caraway seeds
salt and freshly ground pepper to taste
3/4 cup sour cream
1 cup mayonnaise

Serve Artichokes Filled with Chicken Salad with a crusty French bread. The flavors of the artichoke and the salad are too delicate for sourdough or seasoned bread.

Artichokes Filled with Chicken Salad

Artichokes
juice of ½ lemon
2 tablespoons olive oil
4 cups water
2 large cloves of garlic
1 bay leaf
1 teaspoon (scant) salt
4 to 6 artichokes

Chicken Salad
1 cup salad oil
½ to ⅔ cup red wine
    vinegar
1 tablespoon (scant) sugar
1 teaspoon salt
freshly ground pepper to
    taste
4 cups chopped cooked
    chicken
½ to 1 cup chopped green
    onions
1 cup (about) mayonnaise
1 cup chopped celery
1 tablespoon dried tarragon

Garnish
green onions or parsley

For the artichokes, combine the lemon juice, olive oil, water, garlic, bay leaf and salt in a large saucepan. Add the artichokes, coating well. Bring to a boil over high heat and reduce the heat to medium-low. Cook, covered, for 45 minutes or until the artichokes are tender but still firm when the bottom is tested with a fork. Invert to drain and cool.

Pull aside the outer leaves and remove only the soft center leaves; scrape the choke gently away from the heart. Chill until serving time.

For the salad, combine the oil, vinegar, sugar, salt and pepper in a bowl and mix well. Add the chicken. Chill for 1 hour or longer. Add the green onions, mayonnaise, celery and tarragon; mix well. Let stand for 1 hour.

Spoon the salad into the cavities of the artichokes at serving time. Garnish with green onions or parsley.

Serves Four to Six

Spring

Try substituting marinated grilled chicken for the shrimp in this dish or vary the vegetables according to what is seasonally available.

Pinon's Shrimp and Pasta Salad

For the vinaigrette, combine the garlic, cilantro, mustard, lime juice, lime zest, vinegar, salt and pepper in a bowl and mix well. Add the corn oil in a fine stream, whisking constantly until well mixed. Chill until serving time.

For the salad, cook the pasta al dente using the package directions. Rinse under cold water and drain well. Toss with the olive oil in a large bowl.

Add the parsley, cilantro, scallions, carrot, bell peppers, tomatoes, spinach and shrimp to the pasta and mix gently. Add the vinaigrette and toss gently. Correct the seasoning.

Serves Six to Eight

Cilantro Lime Vinaigrette
3 cloves of garlic, minced
1/4 cup minced cilantro
2 tablespoons Dijon
 mustard
juice and zest of 1 lime
1/4 cup white wine vinegar
1 teaspoon salt
1/2 teaspoon pepper
2/3 cup corn oil

Salad
8 ounces uncooked farfalle
 or bow tie pasta
1 tablespoon olive oil
2 tablespoons minced fresh
 parsley
2 tablespoons minced fresh
 cilantro
2 tablespoons minced
 scallions
1/2 cup julienned carrot
1 cup julienned red bell
 pepper
1 cup julienned green bell
 pepper
1 basket cherry tomatoes,
 cut into halves
1 (10-ounce) package fresh
 spinach, torn
1 pound (or more) peeled
 cooked shrimp

Pinon Market and Cafe is a small but mighty neighborhood favorite in Salt Lake City's East Bench area. Chef/owner Victoria Topham is not only a first-class pastry chef; she and her staff also offer a complete menu of super-fresh flavorful salads, sandwiches, pizzas, and daily specials. Pinon is much sought after for catering, but if you just want a cup of coffee and a state-of-the-art fresh herb muffin, this is also the place. It is Victoria's passion for quality and freshness that keeps people coming back for items, such as her Shrimp and Pasta Salad with cilantro lime vinaigrette.

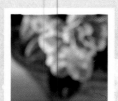

Pacific Rim Glazed Flank Steak

Ingredients
1 cup prepared teriyaki
   marinade
1/2 cup chopped onion
1 large clove of garlic,
   minced
1/3 cup honey
1/3 cup fresh orange juice
1 tablespoon dark sesame
   oil
1 tablespoon chopped fresh
   rosemary
pepper to taste
1 (1 1/2- to 2-pound) flank
   steak

Garnish
orange slices
rosemary sprigs

Combine the teriyaki marinade, onion, garlic, honey, orange juice, sesame oil, rosemary and pepper in a shallow medium dish; whisk to mix well. Remove and reserve 3/4 cup of the mixture for basting.

Score both sides of the steak with a sharp knife. Place in the remaining marinade in the dish. Marinate, covered, in the refrigerator for 30 minutes, turning once.

Drain and discard the marinade. Place the steak on a grill over medium ash-covered coals. Grill for 17 to 21 minutes for medium-rare to medium, basting occasionally with the reserved marinade and turning once.

Place any remaining marinade in a saucepan on the grill and bring to a boil. Boil for 5 minutes. Slice the steak diagonally into thin slices. Spoon hot marinade over the slices.

Garnish with orange slices and rosemary.

Serves Four to Six

Sirloin Pasta with Portobello Mushrooms

Cook the pasta using the package directions; drain and keep warm.

Cut the sirloin slices into halves lengthwise and then crosswise into strips 1 inch wide. Heat 1 to 2 tablespoons olive oil in a large nonstick skillet over medium-high heat. Add the beef and garlic $1/2$ at a time. Stir-fry for 1 to 2 minutes or until the outside is no longer pink; remove with a slotted spoon. Season with salt and pepper.

Heat 1 tablespoon olive oil in the same skillet. Add the mushrooms and bell peppers. Stir-fry for 3 to 4 minutes or until the mushrooms are tender.

Return the beef to the skillet. Sprinkle with the flour and stir to mix well. Stir in the water and beef bouillon. Simmer, covered, for 3 minutes or until thickened, stirring frequently. Stir in the basil.

Spoon the pasta onto serving plates. Spoon the beef over the top. Sprinkle with the cheese.

Serves Four

Ingredients

8 ounces uncooked linguine

1 to $1^{1}/_{4}$ pounds sirloin steak, trimmed, thinly sliced

1 to 2 tablespoons olive oil

2 large cloves of garlic, crushed

$1/2$ teaspoon salt

$1/2$ teaspoon pepper

1 tablespoon olive oil

8 ounces portobello mushroom caps, sliced $1/4$ inch thick

$1/2$ medium red bell pepper, sliced into $1/8$-inch strips

$1/2$ medium yellow bell pepper, sliced into $1/8$-inch strips

2 tablespoons flour

1 cup water

1 teaspoon instant beef bouillon

2 tablespoons thinly sliced fresh basil

$1/3$ cup grated Romano cheese

Glazed ham makes a beautiful centerpiece for an Easter or holiday buffet.

Glazed Ham with Poached Orange Slices

Poached Oranges
2 small thin-skinned
　oranges
1 cup sugar
2 cups water

Ham
1 (10- to 12-pound)
　partially-cooked bone-in
　ham, at room
　temperature
2 to 3 cups Madeira
3/4 cup packed brown sugar
whole cloves (optional)

For the poached oranges, cut the oranges crosswise into 7 or 8 slices, discarding the end pieces and seeds. Poach in boiling water in a saucepan for 1 minute; drain and set aside. Bring the sugar and 2 cups water to a boil in the same saucepan, stirring to dissolve the sugar. Reduce the heat and add the orange slices. Simmer, uncovered, for 5 minutes. Cool the slices in the cooking liquid.

For the ham, place an oven rack in the lower third of an oven preheated to 350 degrees. Wipe the ham with a damp cloth and place fat side down on a rack in a roasting pan. Roast for 1 1/2 hours or to 130 degrees on a meat thermometer, basting frequently with the wine. Remove from the oven and turn fat side up.

Blend the brown sugar with enough wine to make a thick paste. Spread on top of the ham. Roast for 30 to 45 minutes longer or to 160 degrees on a meat thermometer, basting 2 or 3 times with pan juices and remaining wine.

Remove the ham to a platter and top with orange slices, securing with whole cloves. Let stand for 10 minutes before carving. Include an orange slice with each serving.

Serves Eight to Ten

Grilled Pork Tenderloin with Spice Rub

Mix the garlic, thyme, sage, allspice, salt and pepper in a small bowl. Rub on the pork tenderloin and let stand for 30 minutes. Grill over medium coals for about 20 minutes, turning occasionally; do not overcook.

Serves Six

Ingredients
2 cloves of garlic, minced
2 tablespoons chopped
  fresh thyme, or
  2 teaspoons dried
1 tablespoon chopped fresh
  sage, or 1 teaspoon dried
1/4 teaspoon ground
  allspice or cloves
2 teaspoons salt
1 teaspoon ground pepper
2 1/2 pound pork tenderloin

Spring Mint Lamb Chops

Mix the olive oil, garlic, mint, cumin, coriander, salt, cayenne and black pepper in a small bowl. Spread over both sides of the lamb chops.

Grill the lamb chops for 4 to 5 minutes on each side or until brown and crusty on the outside but still pink on the inside; turn only once. Remove to a serving platter.

Garnish with mint sprigs.

Substitute 8 lamb loin chops for the 4 large lamb chops if preferred.

Serves Four

Ingredients
1/4 cup olive oil
4 large cloves of garlic,
  crushed
1/4 cup chopped fresh mint
2 teaspoons ground cumin
1 teaspoon ground
  coriander
1 teaspoon salt
1/2 teaspoon cayenne
1 teaspoon black pepper
4 large lamb chops

Garnish
fresh mint sprigs

Lamb Burgers with Yogurt Dill Sauce

Yogurt Dill Sauce
8 ounces plain yogurt
2 tablespoons finely
    chopped onion
2 tablespoons finely
    chopped mint
1 tablespoon sugar
1 tablespoon dried
    dillweed
1/4 teaspoon salt
1/4 teaspoon white pepper

Lamb Burgers
2 pounds ground lamb
1 large egg
1 large clove of garlic,
    minced
1/2 cup minced onion
1/4 cup chopped fresh mint,
    or 1 tablespoon dried
2 tablespoons chopped
    fresh oregano, or
    1 teaspoon dried
1 teaspoon salt
1/4 teaspoon pepper
4 pita bread rounds, cut
    into halves
2 tomatoes, coarsely
    chopped
1 onion, thinly sliced
1 green bell pepper, thinly
    sliced

For the sauce, combine the yogurt, onion, mint, sugar, dillweed, salt and white pepper in a small bowl and mix well. Chill, covered, for 1 hour or longer.

For the lamb burgers, combine the ground lamb, egg, garlic, onion, mint, oregano, salt and pepper in a bowl and mix well. Shape into 8 burgers 1/2 inch thick and 3 inches in diameter. Grill over medium coals or brown in olive oil in a skillet for 4 to 5 minutes on each side.

To serve the burgers, place each burger in half a pita round. Add tomatoes, onion, green pepper and sauce to each sandwich. Serve immediately.

Serves Eight

Paintbrush
Albion Basin, Wasatch National Forest

Classic Chicken Piccata is a very flexible recipe that can be easily adjusted. Add more or less lemon juice or peel, omit capers, or add more cheese—whatever you like. It's also easy to double and makes an excellent dinner party dish with rice pilaf and steamed fresh asparagus.

Classic Chicken Piccata

Ingredients
1 teaspoon paprika
¹/₃ cup flour
4 boneless skinless chicken
  breasts
1 tablespoon olive oil
¹/₄ cup water
¹/₄ cup lemon juice
1 tablespoon instant
  chicken bouillon
1 tablespoon lemon juice
1 teaspoon grated lemon
  peel
¹/₄ cup milk
¹/₄ cup water
1 tablespoon flour
¹/₄ teaspoon garlic powder
1 tablespoon capers
¹/₂ cup shredded Swiss
  cheese

Mix the paprika and ¹/₃ cup flour in a plastic bag. Add the chicken 1 or 2 pieces at a time and shake to coat lightly.

Brown the chicken on both sides in the olive oil in a large skillet. Add ¹/₄ cup water and ¹/₄ cup lemon juice. Reduce the heat and simmer, covered, for 10 minutes or until tender. Remove to a baking dish, reserving the pan juices in the skillet.

Combine the chicken bouillon, 1 tablespoon lemon juice, lemon peel, milk, ¹/₄ cup water, 1 tablespoon flour and garlic powder in a bowl and mix well. Pour into the skillet. Bring just to the simmering point over medium heat; do not boil. Stir in the capers. Pour over the chicken.

Bake the chicken, covered, at 350 degrees for 15 minutes. Sprinkle with the cheese. Bake, uncovered, for 2 to 3 minutes longer or until the cheese melts.

Serves Four

Bit and Spur Pollo Relleno

For the salsa, cut the pineapple into 1-inch pieces. Combine with the onion, jalapeño pepper, Anaheim pepper, bell pepper, cilantro, chili powder and cumin in a bowl and mix well. Set aside.

For the pesto, combine the cilantro, Parmesan cheese, walnuts, garlic, salt and pepper in a food processor container. Pulse until chopped. Add the olive oil gradually, processing to form a smooth paste. Combine with the goat cheese in a bowl and mix well.

For the glazed chicken, combine the honey, wine and chili powder in a small saucepan. Cook until heated through.

Cut a horizontal slit in each chicken breast to form a pocket. Fill the pocket with the pesto mixture. Grill the chicken until nearly cooked through. Brush with the honey glaze. Grill the chicken until cooked through.

To serve, place the chicken on individual serving plates. Top with the salsa. Garnish with cilantro sprigs.

Serves Six

Pineapple Salsa
1 fresh pineapple
1 red onion, finely chopped
1 fresh jalapeño pepper, finely minced
1 fresh Anaheim or poblano pepper, minced
1 red bell pepper, chopped
1/2 bunch cilantro, chopped
1 teaspoon chili powder
1/2 teaspoon ground cumin

Cilantro Pesto
3 bunches fresh cilantro
1 cup grated Parmesan cheese
1 cup walnuts or pine nuts
1 tablespoon minced garlic
salt and pepper to taste
1/4 to 1/2 cup olive oil
6 ounces fresh goat cheese, crumbled

Glazed Chicken
1/4 cup honey
1 tablespoon red wine
1 teaspoon chili powder
6 (8-ounce) boneless skinless chicken breasts

Garnish
cilantro sprigs

The Bit and Spur Restaurant and Saloon is a real find in Springdale, the small but culinarily sophisticated town just outside Zion National Park. The original owners, described as "gentlemen ski bums," moved there in 1981 to thaw out and try something new. In the process, they found a little pool and beer hall that was ripe for change. They kept one pool table but turned the rest of the place into a music-filled restaurant known for its own refined versions of Mexican-Southwestern food. Owner Joe Jennings and his partner/chef Randall Richards credit former chef Michael Perry, a Hurricane, Utah, native, for many of their favorite recipes. This one is typical of the creative fare that keeps drawing visitors back to the restaurant.

*Once you've got the chicken in the spice-laced yogurt marinade,
the rest of this recipe is easy.*

Sundial Peak Tandoori Chicken

Ingredients

2 medium onions, chopped

2 cloves of garlic

6 tablespoons salad oil

¼ cup lemon juice

2 tablespoons minced
   peeled ginger

2 teaspoons sugar

1 tablespoon ground
   coriander

1 teaspoon ground cumin

1 teaspoon turmeric

½ teaspoon ground
   cardamom

4 teaspoons salt

½ teaspoon cayenne

½ cup plain yogurt

2 (3-pound) chickens, cut
   into quarters

Combine the onions, garlic, oil, lemon juice, ginger, sugar, coriander, cumin, turmeric, cardamom, salt and cayenne in a blender container. Process until smooth. Pour into a shallow dish and stir in the yogurt. Remove some of the yogurt mixture for basting and refrigerate.

Cut diagonal slashes in the chicken, stopping short of the bone. Add to the marinade, coating well. Marinate in the refrigerator for 12 hours or longer, turning the chicken occasionally.

To grill the chicken, remove it from the marinade and place on a heated grill over low coals; discard the marinade. Grill the chicken for 35 minutes or until cooked through, basting frequently with the reserved yogurt mixture.

To broil the chicken, remove it from the marinade and place it skin side down in a broiling pan; discard the marinade. Baste the chicken with the reserved yogurt mixture. Broil 7 to 9 inches from the heat source for 25 minutes or until golden brown. Turn the chicken and baste again. Broil for 15 minutes longer or until cooked through.

Serves Eight

Form this salmon mixture into bite-size balls to serve on an hors d'oeuvre tray with wooden picks and a dipping sauce. The bread crumbs should be made with fresh bread in a blender or food processor.

Salmon Cakes

Combine the parsley, green onions and shallots in a food processor and process until finely chopped. Add $1^1/_2$ cups bread crumbs, eggs, butter, mayonnaise, mustard and lemon juice; pulse to mix well. Add the salmon and pulse just until mixed; do not overmix. Season with salt and pepper.

Shape the mixture into 12 cakes. Coat with $1^1/_2$ cups bread crumbs. Sauté in the oil in a skillet over medium heat until golden brown on both sides.

Serves Six

Ingredients
$1/_3$ cup chopped parsley
4 green onions
3 shallots
$1^1/_2$ cups fresh white bread
  crumbs
2 eggs
2 tablespoons melted
  unsalted butter
2 tablespoons mayonnaise
1 tablespoon prepared
  mustard
2 teaspoons lemon juice
$2^1/_2$ cups (15 ounces) flaked
  cooked salmon
salt and pepper to taste
$1^1/_2$ cups fresh white bread
  crumbs
$1/_2$ cup vegetable oil

Rice vinegar, soy sauce, and sesame oil add a nice Asian flavor profile to the marinade for the season's first barbecue. It makes a full meal served with basmati or jasmine rice sprinkled with chopped cilantro.

Grilled Swordfish with Spring Vegetables

Spring Vegetables
2 teaspoons red wine vinegar
1 teaspoon rice vinegar
1/4 cup reduced-sodium soy sauce
1/2 cup olive oil
1 tablespoon roasted sesame oil
2 teaspoons black sesame seeds or poppy seeds
2 teaspoons white sesame seeds
1/2 teaspoon minced garlic
6 basil leaves, julienned
32 (or more) very thin asparagus spears
salt to taste
1 cup julienned snow peas

Swordfish
1/2 cup olive oil
salt and pepper to taste
4 (7-ounce) swordfish steaks, 1 1/2 inches thick

Garnish
basil sprigs

For the vegetables, combine the wine vinegar, rice vinegar, soy sauce, olive oil, sesame oil, sesame seeds, garlic and basil in a wide shallow bowl; mix well.

Blanch the asparagus in boiling salted water in a saucepan for 3 minutes. Drain the asparagus and plunge into ice water until cool; drain. Add the asparagus and snow peas to the vinaigrette and mix to coat well. Chill until serving time.

For the swordfish, combine the olive oil, salt and pepper in a shallow dish. Add the swordfish. Marinate for 15 minutes or longer; drain. Grill the swordfish for 3 minutes on each side or until cooked through but still moist on the inside.

To serve, place the vegetables on individual serving plates. Place the swordfish steaks on the vegetables. Garnish with basil sprigs.

Serves Four

Black Bean and Goat Cheese Enchiladas

For the salsa, combine the chicken broth, tomatillos, garlic, onion and serrano pepper in a saucepan. Cook over medium-high heat for 10 minutes, stirring frequently. Combine with the cilantro in a food processor and process until smooth. Set aside.

For the beans, combine the chicken broth, beans, garlic, serrano pepper, mango, scallions and corn in a medium saucepan. Bring to a boil and whisk in the goat cheese. Season with salt.

For the tortillas, heat the corn oil in a skillet until smoking. Add the tortillas 1 at a time and cook just until moistened and sealed. Drain between paper towels.

To prepare the enchiladas, spoon the bean mixture down the center of each tortilla. Roll the tortillas to enclose the bean mixture and place seam side down on serving plates. Spoon the salsa over the top and garnish with red bell pepper.

Substitute fresh or canned green tomatoes if tomatillos are not available.

Serves Four

Tomatillo Salsa
1/2 cup chicken broth
4 or 5 tomatillos, husks removed, chopped
2 cloves of garlic
1/2 cup chopped yellow onion
1 serrano pepper, seeded
1 tablespoon chopped fresh cilantro

Black Beans
1/4 cup chicken broth
1 cup cooked black beans
1 clove of garlic, minced
1 serrano pepper, minced
1/4 cup chopped fresh mango or papaya
2 scallions, white part only, thinly sliced
1/4 cup corn kernels (optional)
1/4 cup goat cheese
salt to taste

Tortillas
1/4 cup corn oil
4 (6-inch) corn tortillas

Garnish
1/2 cup chopped red bell pepper

Cache Valley Cheese Soufflé

Ingredients
¼ cup flour
3 tablespoons melted butter
1 cup (scant) milk
¾ cup shredded cheese
salt and cayenne to taste
3 egg yolks
4 egg whites

Blend the flour into the butter in a saucepan. Cook until bubbly, stirring constantly. Stir in the milk. Cook until thickened, stirring constantly. Add the cheese, stirring until melted. Remove from the heat and season with salt and cayenne. Stir a small amount of the hot mixture into the egg yolks; stir the eggs yolks into the hot mixture. Keep warm.

Beat the egg whites until stiff peaks form. Add 1 tablespoon of the egg whites to the cooked mixture. Fold the remainder of the egg whites gently into the cooked mixture. Adjust the seasonings. Spoon into a buttered and floured 5- to 6-inch soufflé dish.

Place in an oven that has been preheated to 425 degrees. Reduce the oven temperature to 400 degrees. Bake for 20 to 25 minutes or until brown and puffed but still moist in the center.

Be sure that everyone is seated with forks in hand and serve immediately.

Serves Four

Some people are surprised to learn that Utah is home to acres of lush dairy land, much of it in Cache Valley, in northern Utah. It's home to the nation's largest Swiss cheese factory.

Asparagus Italian Style

Combine the olive oil, lemon juice, lemon peel, sugar, salt, and half the Parmesan cheese in a bowl and mix well.

Trim the asparagus and peel with a vegetable peeler. Place in a shallow pan and cover half-way with water. Simmer for 8 minutes or until tender-crisp. Drain and rinse under cold water.

Pat the asparagus dry with a paper towel. Arrange on a serving platter lined with lettuce or red cabbage. Pour the olive oil mixture over the top. Sprinkle with pepper and the remaining Parmesan cheese. Serve chilled or at room temperature.

To grill the asparagus, marinate it in the olive oil mixture for 1 hour. Place directly on the grill or on a sheet of foil and grill for several minutes on both sides.

Serves Four to Six

Ingredients
¹/₂ cup extra-virgin olive oil
juice and grated peel of
    1 lemon
sugar and salt to taste
¹/₄ cup grated Parmesan
    cheese
15 to 20 stalks asparagus
lettuce or red cabbage
¹/₂ tablespoon freshly
    cracked pepper

Many chefs prefer thick asparagus stalks over thin, saying they have more flavor. In either case, choose stalks that are slightly firm with compact tips, and cook them as soon as possible. Trim stalks where they snap easily. Peel the ends with a vegetable peeler if you like.

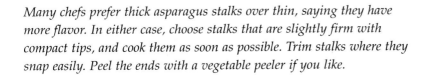

Fresh Peas with Lemon Zest

Ingredients
1 pound fresh peas, or
   1 (10-ounce) package
   frozen peas, thawed
2 tablespoons butter
grated lemon zest

Cook the peas in boiling water in a saucepan for 3 minutes or until tender; drain. Add the butter and toss gently. Spoon into a serving bowl and top with the lemon zest.

Serves Four

Baby New Potatoes

Ingredients
3 pounds small red new
   potatoes
¼ cup melted butter or
   margarine
2 tablespoons chopped
   parsley
¼ teaspoon salt
⅛ teaspoon pepper

Combine the potatoes with cold water to cover in a large saucepan. Bring to a boil and cook for 10 to 15 minutes or until tender; drain. Cut the potatoes into halves and place in a serving bowl. Drizzle with the butter and sprinkle with the parsley, salt and pepper; toss gently to mix well.

Serves Eight

Potatoes Gratin

Spray a 10-inch gratin dish or shallow baking dish 3 times with nonstick cooking spray. Layer 1/3 of the potatoes in an overlapping spiral in the dish. Sprinkle with 1 tablespoon flour and top with the onion rings. Sprinkle with the cayenne and 1/2 teaspoon paprika.

Arrange half the remaining potatoes in a spiral over the layers. Sprinkle with 1 tablespoon flour, the black pepper and 1 tablespoon Parmesan cheese. Add the zucchini and sprinkle with the nutmeg and Spike seasoning. Top with the remaining potatoes.

Pour the evaporated milk over the layers. Sprinkle with 1/2 teaspoon paprika and 1 tablespoon Parmesan cheese. Bake, covered with foil, at 400 degrees for 45 minute. Reduce the oven temperature to 350 degrees and bake, uncovered, for 15 minutes longer or until golden brown. Let stand for 10 minutes before serving. Garnish with parsley.

Serves Eight

Ingredients

3 medium baking potatoes, thinly sliced
1 tablespoon flour
1 medium onion, thinly sliced into rings
1/8 teaspoon cayenne
1/2 teaspoon paprika
1 tablespoon flour
1/2 teaspoon freshly ground black pepper
1 tablespoon grated Parmesan cheese
1 small zucchini, thinly sliced
1/4 teaspoon nutmeg
1/2 teaspoon Spike seasoning
1 (12-ounce) can evaporated skim milk
1/2 teaspoon paprika
1 tablespoon grated Parmesan cheese

Garnish

2 tablespoons chopped fresh parsley

Broccoli, cauliflower, green beans, and asparagus are best blanched before using in salad or serving as crudités. Cook them in boiling water for about one minute and rinse with cold water to stop the cooking.

Color Country Vegetables

Ingredients

8 medium beets with tops
9 baby turnips with tops, or
   3 medium turnips
salt to taste
18 baby carrots with tops,
   or 3 large carrots
12 ounces mixed red and
   yellow pearl onions
3 tablespoons unsalted
   butter
salt and pepper to taste
1 tablespoon olive oil
1/4 cup loosely packed fresh
   flat-leaf parsley

Preheat the oven to 425 degrees. Trim the beets, leaving 1-inch stems. Wrap them tightly in foil and place in a baking pan. Roast for 1 to 1 1/2 hours or until tender. Unwrap and allow to cool. Slip off and discard the skins. Cut each beet into 6 wedges.

Trim the baby turnips, leaving 1/4-inch stems, or peel medium turnips and cut into 6 wedges. Blanch in boiling salted water in a saucepan for 3 to 6 minutes or just until tender. Remove with a slotted spoon to a bowl of ice water to cool. Trim the baby carrots, leaving 1/4-inch stems, or peel large carrots and cut into 1/2x3-inch sticks. Return the saucepan of water to a boil and add the carrots. Blanch for 5 minutes or just until tender. Remove to the bowl of ice water to cool. Drain the turnips and carrots in a colander. Cut baby turnips into halves. Return the saucepan of water to a boil and add the onions. Blanch for 3 minutes or just until tender. Drain in another colander, cool and peel.

Heat the butter in a large nonstick skillet over medium-high heat until the foam subsides. Add the turnips and carrots and season with salt and pepper. Sauté for 4 minutes or until tender and golden brown. Remove with a slotted spoon to a bowl and keep warm.

Add the olive oil to the skillet and heat until hot but not smoking. Add the onions and season with salt and pepper. Sauté for 4 minutes or until tender and golden brown. Remove to the bowl with the turnips and carrots. Add the parsley to the vegetables and mix lightly.

Add the beets to the oil in the skillet and season with salt and pepper. Sauté until heated through. Add to the bowl of vegetables but do not mix.

Serves Six

Enjoy a melange of vegetables as colorful as the Utah region dubbed "color country." The region includes the sunset hues of Zion and Bryce Canyon National Parks as well as the Dixie National Forest and the red and yellow of the new Grand Staircase Escalante National Monument.

"Sweating" is a method by which vegetables are rendered very tender and translucent but not brown by heating very slowly in oil or butter in a heavy pot. For best results, cover the ingredients directly with parchment or waxed paper and cover tightly.

Log Haven Carrot Risotto

Melt the butter in a heavy saucepan. Add the onion, celery and garlic and sweat until very tender and translucent. Stir in the rice. Sauté until the grains turn white. Add the wine and cook for several minutes, stirring constantly.

Add the hot vegetable stock 1 cup at a time, cooking until the liquid is absorbed after each addition. Stir in the carrot juice, cream and lemon thyme. Cook until all the liquid is absorbed. Season to taste with nutmeg, salt and pepper. Garnish with the chopped parsley and serve immediately.

You may finish this dish with ¼ cup Brie or Parmesan cheese if desired.

Serves Six

Ingredients
2 tablespoons butter
1 small onion, chopped
3 ribs celery, chopped
4 cloves of garlic, finely
 minced
1½ cups uncooked arborio
 rice
½ cup white wine
2 cups hot vegetable stock
1 cup carrot juice
¼ cup cream
6 sprigs lemon thyme,
 chopped
nutmeg, salt and pepper
 to taste

Garnish
½ bunch parsley, chopped

Spring

Log Haven restaurant is an elegantly restored 100-year-old log home in Millcreek Canyon, just about 25 minutes from downtown Salt Lake City. Chef David Jones has made his mark there as one of Utah's most creative and artistic cooks. He likes to serve this risotto with glazed duck, but it's also excellent with pork chops, roasted chicken, game hens, or just by itself as a vegetarian entrée.

Lemon Rice

Melt the butter in a medium saucepan. Add the rice and sauté for several minutes. Add the chicken broth, lemon juice, turmeric, salt and pepper. Bring to a boil and reduce the heat.

Simmer, covered, for 30 minutes or until most of the liquid is absorbed. Simmer, uncovered, for 5 minutes longer or until the liquid is absorbed and the rice is tender.

Serves Six to Eight

Ingredients
6 tablespoons butter
1 cup uncooked converted
    rice
2 cups chicken broth
3 to 4 tablespoons fresh
    lemon juice
1/8 teaspoon turmeric
salt and pepper to taste

Asparagus Risotto with Saffron

Bring the vegetable broth to a boil in a heavy medium saucepan. Add the asparagus. Cook for 2 minutes or until tender-crisp. Remove to a bowl with a slotted spoon.

Add the wine and saffron to the vegetable broth and bring to a simmer; keep warm.

Heat the olive oil in a second heavy medium saucepan. Add the rice and sauté for 2 minutes or until translucent. Stir in all but 1/4 cup of the broth mixture. Simmer, uncovered, for 20 minutes or until the rice is tender but still slightly firm, stirring occasionally.

Stir in the peas, asparagus and cheese. Add the remaining 1/4 cup broth if necessary for the desired consistency. Season with salt and pepper.

Serves Two

Ingredients
3 cups vegetable broth
8 ounces slender
    asparagus, cut into
    1-inch pieces
1 cup dry white wine
1/4 teaspoon saffron threads
1 1/2 tablespoons olive oil
1 cup arborio rice,
    or medium-grain
    white rice
1 cup frozen tiny peas,
    thawed
1/3 cup grated Parmesan
    cheese
salt and pepper to taste

Evening Primrose
Antelope Island State Park, Great Salt Lake

Almond Breakfast Pastry

Almond Topping
1 cup water
¹/₂ cup margarine
1 cup flour
¹/₄ teaspoon salt
3 or 4 eggs
1¹/₂ teaspoons almond
   extract

Pastry
¹/₂ cup margarine
1 cup flour
2 tablespoons cold water

Almond Frosting
¹/₂ cup butter, softened
1 egg or egg substitute
1¹/₂ teaspoons almond
   extract
2 cups confectioners' sugar

Garnish
1 cup slivered almonds

For the topping, mix the water and margarine in a saucepan and bring to a boil. Remove from the heat. Stir in the flour and salt. Beat in the eggs 1 at a time. Add the almond extract. Set aside.

For the pastry, mix the margarine into the flour in a bowl with a fork until the mixture has the texture of cornmeal. Add the cold water and mix to form a dough. Divide the dough into halves. Pat each half into a 3x12-inch rectangle on an ungreased baking sheet. Spread the topping over the pastry strips.

Place the baking sheets on the middle rack of an oven preheated to 350 degrees. Bake for 45 minutes. Cool to room temperature.

For the frosting, combine the butter, egg and almond extract in a bowl and beat until smooth. Add the confectioners' sugar; mix well. Spread over the cooled pastries. Garnish with the almonds.

Serves Eight

Lemon Raisin Muffins

Combine the all-purpose flour, whole wheat flour, brown sugar, baking powder, baking soda and salt in a bowl and mix well. Make a well in the center.

Combine the yogurt, margarine, egg whites, lemon juice, lemon peel and vanilla in a bowl and mix well. Stir in the raisins. Add to the well in the dry ingredients and mix just until moistened.

Spoon into 12 paper-lined muffin cups. Bake at 400 degrees for 15 to 20 minutes or until a wooden pick inserted in the center comes out clean. Remove to a wire rack to cool.

Makes One Dozen

Ingredients
2 cups all-purpose flour
$1/4$ cup whole wheat flour
$1/3$ cup packed brown sugar
1 teaspoon baking powder
1 teaspoon baking soda
$1/4$ teaspoon salt
1 cup nonfat vanilla yogurt
$1/4$ cup melted margarine
2 egg whites
2 tablespoons lemon juice
2 tablespoons grated lemon
    peel
1 teaspoon vanilla extract
$3/4$ cup raisins

Chez Betty's Housemade Corn Muffins

Mix the cornmeal, flour, sugar, baking powder and salt in a bowl. Add the oil and milk and mix just until moistened.

Spoon into miniature muffin cups sprayed with nonstick cooking spray, filling $1/2$ full. Bake at 350 degrees for 13 to 15 minutes or until golden brown.

Makes Two Dozen

Ingredients
$2/3$ cup cornmeal
$1 1/4$ cups flour
$1/3$ cup sugar
1 tablespoon baking
    powder
$1/2$ teaspoon salt
$1/3$ cup canola oil
1 cup milk

Chez Betty restaurant in Park City is a long-time favorite of diners from all over the world. One reason might just be the signature corn muffins Chef Jerry Garcia bakes every night. They're light and airy—and great straight from the oven.

Country Buttermilk Scones

Ingredients
3 cups flour
$1/3$ cup sugar
$2^{1}/_{2}$ teaspoons baking
   powder
$1/2$ teaspoon baking soda
$3/4$ teaspoon salt
$3/4$ cup butter or margarine
$3/4$ cup currants
1 teaspoon grated orange
   zest (optional)
1 cup buttermilk
1 egg, beaten

Mix the flour, sugar, baking powder, baking soda and salt in a large bowl. Add the butter and blend with a fork or pastry blender until the mixture has the texture of coarse cornmeal. Stir in the currants and orange zest. Add the buttermilk and stir with a fork until the dough pulls away from the side of the bowl.

Shape into a ball on a lightly floured surface. Divide into 3 portions and roll each portion into a circle $1/2$ inch thick. Cut each circle into 6 wedges. Place $1^{1}/_{2}$ inches apart on lightly greased baking sheets. Brush the tops with egg.

Bake at 425 degrees for 12 to 15 minutes on until the tops are golden brown. Serve warm with preserves and butter or whipped cream.

Makes One and One-Half Dozen

Easy Chocolate Cake

Combine the chocolate and butter in a heavy medium saucepan. Heat over low heat until melted, stirring to mix well.

Beat the eggs and sugar in a large bowl until smooth and thickened. Sift the flour and baking powder over the egg mixture and fold in gently. Fold in the chocolate mixture gradually.

Spoon into a buttered and floured springform pan with a 2^3/$_4$-inch side. Bake at 325 degrees for 20 minutes. Cover with foil. Bake for 30 minutes longer or until a tester inserted into the center comes out with moist crumbs attached.

Remove the foil and cool in the pan on a wire rack; cake will fall as it cools. Run a knife around the edge of the pan to loosen the cake. Place on a serving plate and remove the side of the pan. Garnish with confectioners' sugar.

Serves Ten

Ingredients
10 ounces bittersweet or
    semisweet chocolate,
    chopped
1 cup butter, chopped
5 eggs
1^1/$_4$ cups sugar
5 tablespoons flour
1^1/$_2$ teaspoons baking
    powder

Garnish
confectioners' sugar

Everyone needs a good pound cake recipe. This one, made with whipping cream, is extra moist. Serve it with spring strawberries or the first of the Bear Lake raspberries.

Whipping Cream Cake

Cream the butter and sugar in a mixer bowl until light and fluffy. Add the eggs, flour and whipping cream and mix well. Stir in the flavorings.

Spoon into a greased and floured bundt pan. Bake at 325 degrees for 1¼ hours or until the cake tests done. Cool in the pan for several minutes. Invert onto a wire rack to cool completely.

Garnish with confectioners' sugar and fresh berries.

Serves Sixteen

Ingredients
1 cup butter, softened
3 cups sugar
6 eggs
3 cups cake flour, sifted
1 cup heavy whipping
    cream
1 teaspoon vanilla extract
1 teaspoon lemon extract

Garnish
confectioners' sugar
fresh berries or fruit

52

Named for the Russian ballet dancer Anna Pavlova, this is a classic Australian dessert. It consists of a whipped cream-filled meringue topped by lush fruits of the season.

Pavlova

Draw a 7-inch circle on waxed paper or baking parchment and place on a baking sheet.

Beat the egg whites in a mixer bowl until soft peaks form. Add the sugar gradually, beating constantly until very stiff peaks form. Beat in the vanilla, vinegar and cornstarch. Spread or pipe the mixture inside the circle, forming a depression in the center.

Bake at 300 degrees for 1 hour or until firm. Turn off the oven, leaving the meringue to cool in the oven. Invert the meringue and remove the waxed paper. Place right side up on a serving plate.

For the best results, the cream should be whipped just before serving. Spoon it into the depression in the meringue and arrange the berries on the top to serve. Garnish with mint.

For an optional topping, mix 1 puréed mango with 1 chopped mango and 1 teaspoon of sugar; garnish with sliced kiwifruit.

Serves Six

Ingredients
3 egg whites
6 ounces superfine sugar
½ teaspoon vanilla extract
½ teaspoon vinegar
1 teaspoon cornstarch
10 ounces heavy whipping cream, whipped
1 pint fresh strawberries or raspberries

Garnish
mint sprigs

Rum Raisin Fruit Sauce makes a delicious light dessert served with fresh fruit, but it can also do double duty as an appetizer.

Rum Raisin Fruit Sauce

Ingredients
1 pint sour cream
1½ cups golden raisins
2 tablespoons dark rum
½ cup packed brown sugar
cinnamon and nutmeg
    to taste

Combine the sour cream, raisins, rum, brown sugar, cinnamon and nutmeg in a blender and process until smooth. Chill until serving time. Serve with melons, grapes, pineapple and/or strawberries.

Serves Six to Eight

Lemon Chess Tart

Ingredients
2 tablespoons flour
2 tablespoons cornmeal
1¾ cups sugar
4 eggs
juice and grated peel of
    2 lemons
6 tablespoons melted butter
⅓ cup milk
1 unbaked 9-inch tart shell

Garnish
whipped cream
strawberries, raspberries,
    blueberries or
    pomegranate seeds

Mix the flour, cornmeal and sugar in a mixer bowl. Beat in the eggs 1 at a time. Add the lemon juice, lemon peel, butter and milk and mix well.

   Pour into the tart shell. Bake at 325 degrees for 45 to 60 minutes or until the center no longer moves when the tart is shaken. Cool on a wire rack.

   Garnish with whipped cream and fresh berries or pomegranate seeds.

Serves Ten

Spring

To hull strawberries for garnish, carefully push a plastic drinking straw through each berry from the bottom to the top.

Rhubarb Berry Pie

For the filling, mix the sugar and flour in a large bowl. Add the rhubarb, strawberries and raspberries and mix gently. Chill in the refrigerator for 8 hours or longer. Add the melted butter and lemon juice just before spooning into the pastry.

For the pastry, mix the flour and salt in a bowl. Add the shortening and butter and mix with knives or a pastry blender until the texture resembles coarse cornmeal. Add the water and mix to form a ball. Let stand for 30 minutes or longer.

Divide the dough into halves. Roll 1 half into a circle on a floured surface and place in a pie pan. Spoon the filling into the prepared pan. Roll the remaining dough and fit it over the filling. Seal the edges and cut vents; sprinkle with sugar. Bake at 400 degrees for 10 minutes. Reduce the oven temperature to 350 degrees and bake for 40 to 50 minutes longer or until the crust is golden brown.

Serves Eight

Filling
3/4 cup sugar
1/3 cup flour
2 cups (1/2-inch pieces) rhubarb
1 cup strawberry halves or quarters
1 cup raspberries
1 tablespoon melted butter
1 teaspoon lemon juice

Double-Crust Pastry
2 cups flour
1 teaspoon salt
2/3 cup shortening
2 tablespoons butter
1/4 cup ice water
sugar

Homegrown or wild rhubarb has cherry-red stalks and a stronger flavor than pinkish hothouse rhubarb. In Utah, it's common to find rhubarb in home gardens as well as growing along high mountain streams. Wherever you find it, rhubarb is delicious in combination with lots of sugar and berries, as in this wonderful old-fashioned pie.

Jumbo Chocolate Chip Cookies

Ingredients
$^1/_2$ cup butter, softened
$^1/_2$ cup shortening
$^1/_2$ cup sugar
1 cup packed brown sugar
2 eggs
2 teaspoons vanilla extract
2$^1/_2$ cups flour
1 teaspoon baking soda
$^1/_2$ teaspoon salt
1 (12-ounce) package
    semisweet chocolate
    chips
1 cup chopped pecans or
    walnuts

Cream the butter and shortening in a mixer bowl until light. Add the sugar and brown sugar gradually, beating constantly until fluffy. Beat in the eggs and vanilla.

Mix the flour, baking soda and salt. Add to the creamed mixture and mix well. Stir in the chocolate chips and pecans. Drop by scant $^1/_4$ cupfuls onto ungreased cookie sheets.

Bake at 375 degrees for 10 to 12 minutes or until golden brown. Cool on the cookie sheets for several minutes; remove to a wire rack to cool completely.

You may substitute white chocolate chips and macadamia nuts for the semisweet chocolate chips and pecans if you prefer.

Makes Two Dozen

Picture-Perfect Macaroons

Bring the corn syrup to a boil in a heavy 4-quart saucepan. Swirl the saucepan just above the heat source until bubbles in the liquid are uniform; remove from the heat. Stir in the sugar with a wooden spoon.

Cook until the sugar is dissolved, stirring constantly; mixture will appear grainy and white. Remove from the heat and let stand for 4 minutes. Add the vanilla. Stir in the egg whites vigorously. Add the coconut and cake flour; mix just until the flour is moistened.

Drop by generous tablespoonfuls several inches apart onto nonstick cookie sheets. Bake at 350 degrees for 15 to 20 minutes or until golden brown. Remove immediately to wire racks to cool.

Heat the chocolate with the oil in a double boiler over medium heat until most of the chocolate is melted. Let stand for 5 minutes; stir to blend well. Dip each macaroon into the chocolate, coating $1/3$ of the cookie. Place on waxed paper and let stand until the chocolate is firm.

Makes Three Dozen

Ingredients
$1/2$ cup light corn syrup
$2/3$ cup sugar
2 teaspoons vanilla extract
$3/4$ cup (about 5 large eggs) egg whites, at room temperature
$5 1/3$ cups packed sweetened shredded coconut
$1/3$ cup cake flour, sifted
8 ounces bittersweet or semisweet chocolate
1 teaspoon vegetable oil

Lemon Thyme Crisps are crisp, thin, and perfect with iced tea.
Do not use a substitute for the butter in the recipe.

Lemon Thyme Crisps

Ingredients
3¼ cups flour
2 teaspoons baking soda
½ teaspoon salt
4 teaspoons finely chopped
    fresh lemon thyme or
    thyme
1 cup butter, softened
1½ cups sugar
2½ tablespoons finely
    grated lemon zest
1 large egg
3 tablespoons fresh lemon
    juice
1 tablespoon finely grated
    fresh gingerroot
confectioners' sugar

Sift the flour, baking soda and salt into a bowl. Stir in the thyme. Cream the butter, sugar and lemon zest in a mixer bowl until light and fluffy. Beat in the egg, lemon juice and gingerroot. Add the flour mixture and beat just until moistened.

Divide the dough into halves and shape each into a 1½x14-inch log on waxed paper. Wrap in the waxed paper and foil. Place in the freezer for 20 minutes.

Slice 1 log at a time into ovals ¼ inch thick; cut each slice diagonally into halves. Place 1 inch apart on ungreased cookie sheets.

Bake in batches at 350 degrees for 12 minutes or until golden brown, beginning each batch on a rack in the upper third of the oven and moving it to the lower third after 6 minutes.

Remove cookies immediately to a wire rack to cool. Sprinkle lightly with confectioners' sugar.

Logs may be frozen for up to 3 weeks; allow to come to room temperature before slicing.

Makes Five Dozen

Springtime Tea

Bring 1 cup water to a boil in a saucepan and add the tea bags. Let stand until cool.

Combine the sugar, lemon juice, 4 cups water and flavorings in a saucepan. Bring to a boil and cook for 3 minutes. Let stand until cool. Stir in the steeped tea.

Chill in the refrigerator. Add the ginger ale at serving time.

Serves Six to Eight

Ingredients
1 cup water
6 (regular, decaffeinated or
    herbal) tea bags
2 cups sugar
juice of 4 lemons
4 cups water
1 tablespoon vanilla extract
1 tablespoon almond
    extract
1 quart ginger ale, chilled

Berry Delicious Lemonade

Combine the strawberries, lemon juice and sugar in a blender and process until smooth. Combine with the water, lemon slices and ice in a pitcher.

Serves Six to Eight

Ingredients
1^1/$_2$ cups sliced
    strawberries
1 cup fresh lemon juice
1^1/$_4$ cups sugar
4 cups cold water
1 lemon, sliced
ice

Summer

Outdoor adventures in awesome settings. That pretty much sums up the typical Utahn's summer experience—in addition to countless barbecues, of course. This time of year we're apt to be hiking in the mountains, camping, or looking for petroglyphs in redrock canyons. We're fly-fishing in one of over 1,000 fishable lakes and streams, running rivers, water-skiing, houseboating, bike riding, golfing, or lazing around a pool during those sizzling days when the temperature shoots up over 90 degrees.

Since daytime temperatures in desert canyon areas, such as Arches National Park, often top 110 degrees in midsummer, visitors planning a hike to Delicate Arch are best advised to make it a sunrise or sunset event. As for other evening pastimes, you can't beat stargazing in the Utah deserts and mountains. In places like Desolation Canyon or the 100-mile White Rim Trail, it seems you can practically reach up and touch the Milky Way.

This is the season in which Utah's crops come into their own. Juicy peaches, luscious Bing cherries, pears, apricots, endless supplies of berries from Bear Lake and Paradise, Green River melons, sweet corn, beets, summer squash, homegrown tomatoes, fragrant basil, and mint provide culinary inspiration and lip-smacking satisfaction. We buy them at the farmers' markets, along the Fruit Way near Brigham City, on street corners, and in every market, and we like to enjoy them outdoors whenever possible.

Essentials

Basic Margaritas

Serve fruity margaritas in clear glasses or clear plastic cups to show off their color. Garnish them with skewers of fresh grapes, pineapple, and melon chunks, or simply with mint sprigs.

1/2 cup fresh lime juice
1/4 cup sugar
1/2 cup tequila
2 tablespoons orange liqueur
1 1/2 to 2 cups chopped ice
coarse salt
lime wedges

Combine the lime juice, sugar, tequila, liqueur and ice in a blender container. Process at the highest speed until slushy and evenly mixed.

Spread the salt on a small plate. Rub the rims of the glasses with the lime wedges and dip into the salt to coat well. Pour the margaritas into the salt-rimmed glasses.

For Sorbet Margaritas, omit the sugar; decrease the orange liqueur to 1 tablespoon; substitute 1/2 cup orange juice for the lime juice; and substitute 1 pint of your favorite fruit sorbet for the ice. Add lemon or lime juice 1 tablespoon at a time to adjust the sweetness to your taste.

For Watermelon Margaritas, substitute 4 cups frozen seeded watermelon for the ice. Chop the watermelon into 1-inch pieces and freeze on a baking sheet. Place in plastic bags to store in the freezer. This will prevent the fruit from sticking together. The same method works for berries and grapes.

Star-Spangled Barbecue

Tomato and Fennel Bruschetta

Great Salt Lake Caesar Salad

Café Diablo Pumpkin Seed-Crusted Trout

Corn with Shallot Thyme Butter

Cherry Cobbler with Old-Fashioned Ice Cream

Raspberry Delight Slush

Watermelon Margaritas

Perfect Summer Picnic

Roasted Corn Salsa

Red Rock Dip

Crudités and Pita Wedges

Roasted Chicken Salad with
Bell Pepper and Onion

Brown Sugar Shortbread Cookies

Chocolate-Covered Strawberries with
Grand Marnier

The Best-Ever Lemonade

Cotes du Rhone Blanc

Whether based on corn and tomatoes or tropical fruits and chiles, fresh salsa is so easy to make. Serve it with tortilla chips, as an accompaniment to grilled meats and fish, on hamburgers, as a condiment for chili, over scrambled eggs, or folded into omelets.

Cowboy Caviar

Mix the vinegar, oil, hot sauce, garlic and pepper in a bowl. Cut the avocado into 1/2-inch cubes and add to the vinegar mixture; mixing gently.

Drain and rinse the peas and corn. Add to the vinegar mixture with the cilantro, green onions and tomatoes; mix gently. Add salt to taste.

Serve with tortilla chips.

Serves Ten to Twelve

Ingredients
2 tablespoons red wine
    vinegar
1 1/2 teaspoons salad oil
1 1/2 to 2 teaspoons hot
    sauce
1 clove of garlic, minced
1/8 teaspoon pepper
1 firm ripe avocado
1 (15-ounce) can black-eyed
    peas
1 (11-ounce) can corn, or
    kernels from 2 ears of
    fresh corn, blanched
2/3 cup chopped cilantro
2/3 cup thinly sliced green
    onions
8 ounces Roma tomatoes,
    coarsely chopped
salt to taste

Tomatillo Salsa

Remove the husks from the tomatillos and chop. Combine with the onions, jalapeños, cilantro, olive oil, vinegar, sugar and salt in a saucepan. Simmer for 15 minutes, stirring occasionally.

Process in batches in a food processor. Cool to room temperature. Chill for up to 24 hours to blend flavors. Allow to return to room temperature before serving. Serve with tortilla chips or quesadillas.

Serves Fifteen to Twenty

Ingredients
5 pounds tomatillos
4 yellow onions, chopped
10 jalapeño peppers,
    chopped
3 bunches cilantro,
    chopped
3/4 cup olive oil
1/4 cup cider vinegar
1/2 cup sugar
2 tablespoons salt

*When chiles burn your tongue, cool off with ice cream, milk, or yogurt—
not water. Dairy products contain casein, which washes away
the capsaicin (cap-say-i-sin)—the hot compound found in the veins of
peppers—and lowers the surface temperature of the tongue.*

Roasted Corn Salsa

Trim the ends of the corn and pull back the husks; remove the
silks. Rub the kernels with the olive oil and replace the husks
over the corn. Place on baking sheets. Roast at 450 degrees for
15 minutes, turning after 8 minutes. Cool the corn and cut the
kernels from the cobs.

Combine the corn with the tomatoes, bell peppers, serrano
pepper, onion, basil and lime juice in a bowl and mix well.
Season with sea salt and pepper. Spoon into serving bowls
and serve immediately with chips, or as an accompaniment to
grilled chicken.

Serves Four

Ingredients

2 ears sweet corn with
    husks
2 tablespoons (or more)
    olive oil
2 Roma tomatoes, seeded,
    cut into 1/4-inch pieces
1/4 cup finely chopped red
    bell pepper
1/4 cup finely chopped
    green bell pepper
1 small serrano pepper,
    seeded, minced
1/4 cup finely chopped red
    onion
3 basil leaves, chopped
1 tablespoon fresh lime
    juice
1/4 teaspoon sea salt
1/4 teaspoon fresh ground
    pepper

Summer

*Handle chiles carefully to avoid burns of the hands and eyes. Work
in a ventilated area to avoid respiratory irritation. If you are very
dexterous, hold chiles with the tines of a fork and trim them with a
small sharp knife. Otherwise, work with thin surgical gloves, found at
most pharmacies. If a chile does burn you, rinse the area with rubbing
alcohol, or rinse affected eyes well with water.*

Fruit Salsa

Ingredients

4 plum tomatoes, seeded,
   cut into 1/4-inch pieces
1 cup (1/4-inch pieces)
   cantaloupe
1 cup (1/4-inch pieces)
   watermelon
1 cup (1/4-inch pieces)
   peeled seeded cucumber
1/3 cup chopped red onion
1 teaspoon minced jalapeño
   pepper
2 tablespoons coarsely
   chopped cilantro
2 tablespoons fresh lime
   juice

Combine the tomatoes, cantaloupe, watermelon, cucumber, onion, jalapeño pepper, cilantro and lime juice in a bowl and mix well. Let stand for 1 hour to blend flavors. Serve with chips or as an accompaniment to poultry, fish or fajitas.

For a milder salsa, substitute mild green chiles for the jalapeño.

Serves Twelve

Peachy Black Bean Dip

Ingredients

1 (15-ounce) can black
   beans, drained
3 cups chopped fresh
   peaches
1 cup chopped red onion
2 tablespoons chopped
   cilantro
2 tablespoons olive oil
2 teaspoons cumin
2 teaspoons lime juice
salt and pepper to taste

Combine the beans, peaches, onion and cilantro in a bowl. Add the olive oil, cumin, lime juice, salt and pepper and mix well. Serve immediately or chill in the refrigerator for 8 hours or longer. Serve with tortilla chips or as an accompaniment to grilled fish or chicken.

Substitute 2 chopped fresh mangoes for the peaches for variety; omit the olive oil for a low-fat dip.

Serves Eighteen

Red Rock Dip is a great party recipe, because it can be easily doubled or tripled and made a day in advance.

Red Rock Dip

Sauté the onion and garlic in the olive oil in a skillet over medium heat until tender.

Combine the peppers, basil, bread, lemon juice and walnuts in a food processor and process until the walnuts are finely chopped. Add the onion mixture gradually, processing constantly. Season with salt.

Spoon into a serving dish and serve with toasted pita wedges or wheat thins.

Serves Eight

Ingredients
1 small onion, chopped
2 large cloves of garlic, sliced
¼ cup olive oil
1 (12-ounce) jar roasted red peppers, rinsed, drained
⅓ cup basil leaves
1 slice homemade-type bread, chopped
2 tablespoons lemon juice
½ cup toasted walnuts
salt to taste

Tomato and Fennel Bruschetta

Combine the tomatoes, fennel, basil, olive oil and vinegar in a bowl. Add the salt and pepper and mix well.

Cut the baguette into ½-inch slices. Place on a baking sheet. Broil until toasted golden brown on both sides. Rub the toasted bread with the garlic and let stand until cool. Top with the tomato mixture and serve immediately.

Serves Eight to Twelve

Ingredients
2 large tomatoes, seeded, chopped
½ fennel bulb, trimmed, chopped
¼ cup chopped fresh basil
½ cup plus 2 tablespoons olive oil
1 tablespoon balsamic vinegar
salt and pepper to taste
1 baguette
2 or 3 cloves of garlic, cut into halves

Home gardeners in Utah are passionate about their late-summer vine-ripened tomatoes and fresh herbs. This classic tart makes good use of both tomatoes and oregano in a savory hot appetizer.

Fresh Tomato Tart

Food Processor Pastry
1³/₄ cups flour
1 tablespoon sugar
¹/₂ teaspoon salt
³/₄ cup butter, chilled, chopped
¹/₄ cup ice water

Tart
¹/₃ cup Dijon mustard
8 ounces mozzarella cheese, thinly sliced
10 medium tomatoes, thinly sliced
1 tablespoon garlic
1 tablespoon fresh oregano
salt and pepper to taste
2 tablespoons olive oil

For the pastry, mix the flour, sugar and salt in a food processor container. Add the butter and process until the mixture has the texture of coarse crumbs. Add the water and process until the mixture forms a ball. Place in a bowl and chill, covered, for 30 minutes.

Place the dough on a floured surface. Roll into a circle large enough to fit into a 10-inch tart pan. Fit the pastry into the pan.

For the tart, brush the bottom of the pastry evenly with mustard and arrange the cheese slices evenly over the mustard. Arrange the tomato slices in overlapping circles in the prepared pan beginning at the outer edge. Sprinkle with the garlic, oregano, salt and pepper; drizzle with the olive oil.

Place the tart on a baking sheet. Bake at 400 degrees for 40 minutes or until the crust is golden brown.

Serves Six

Avocado Soup with Papaya Pepper Relish

For the soup, sauté the onion, carrot, celery and garlic in the melted butter in a large saucepan over medium heat for 6 minutes or until tender but not brown. Add the chicken stock. Bring to a boil and remove from the heat. Cool to room temperature. Stir in the cream. Chill for 2 hours or longer.

Add the avocados to the soup and whisk until they begin to break up and thicken the soup. Stir in the lime juice, coriander, salt and pepper. Chill until the flavors blend.

For the relish, roast the bell pepper and poblano pepper over a gas flame or under the boiler until charred on all sides. Place in a paper bag and let stand for 10 minutes to steam. Remove the peel and seed the peppers. Cut into 1/4-inch pieces.

Combine the peppers with the papaya, lime juice and coriander in a bowl and mix well. Stir in the walnut oil, salt and pepper.

Spoon the chilled soup into serving bowls. Top with a dollop of the relish. Garnish with the jalapeño peppers.

Serves Eight to Ten

Soup
1 small onion, minced
1 carrot, minced
2 small ribs of celery, minced
1 clove of garlic, minced
2 teaspoons unsalted butter
4 cups chicken stock
1 cup heavy cream, chilled
2 large Hass or other avocados, cut into 1/4-inch pieces
1 tablespoon lime juice
2 1/2 tablespoons coriander
1/8 teaspoon each salt and pepper

Papaya Pepper Relish
1 small red bell pepper
1 poblano pepper
1 small papaya, peeled, seeded, cut into 1/4-inch pieces
1 tablespoon lime juice
2 1/2 tablespoons coriander
1 teaspoon walnut oil
1/8 teaspoon each salt and pepper

Garnish
3 jalapeño peppers, seeded, minced

Make your own crème fraîche to serve over fresh fruit and desserts, in sauces, or in cream soups. Mix 1 cup whipping cream with 2 tablespoons buttermilk or 1 cup sour cream with 1 to 2 cups heavy cream in a covered jar, and let stand at 70 degrees for 8 to 24 hours or until thick.

Wild Berry Soup

Ingredients
2 cups fresh orange juice
2 slices fresh ginger
¼ cup honey
8 cups assorted fresh
    berries
2 cups heavy cream
8 cups plain yogurt
¾ cup honey
1 cup orange juice

Garnish
crème fraîche
berries

Combine the orange juice, ginger and honey in a small saucepan. Bring to a boil and reduce the heat. Cook until the mixture is reduced by ½.

Purée the berries in a blender. Add the cream, yogurt, honey, orange juice and orange-ginger sauce; process until smooth.

Strain the soup into serving bowls. Garnish with crème fraîche and fresh berries.

Serves Eight

Summer

Chef Mikel Trapp, Food and Beverage Director for the award-winning Stein Eriksen Lodge at Deer Valley Resort, presides over one of the most enviable high-mountain kitchens in Utah. His contemporary menus reflect his classical training as he makes the most of seasonal local ingredients whenever they're available. This cold fruit soup delivers subtle layers of flavor, with fresh ginger and honey peeking through the taste of summer berries and thick heavy cream. Serve it on the hottest of days in shallow white bowls or in wide-mouth goblets with your best silver spoons.

Most of us are familiar with the tomato-based Spanish soup gazpacho. But there is also a range of traditional Scandinavian fruit soups and variations on gazpacho, such as this one.

Cold Tomato Soup with Basil and Walnuts

Peel and seed the tomatoes. Purée half the tomatoes at a time in a food processor. Combine in a glass or ceramic bowl; do not use metal. Add the minced basil, walnut oil, honey, vinegar, salt and pepper and mix well. Adjust the seasonings.

Chill the mixture, covered, in the refrigerator for 3 hours or longer. Spoon into serving bowls. Top with the walnuts and garnish with the basil sprigs.

You may substitute 2 drained 28-ounce cans Italian plum tomatoes for the fresh tomatoes if preferred.

Serves Six

Ingredients
3 pounds fresh tomatoes
1/3 cup minced fresh basil
2 tablespoons walnut oil
1 teaspoon honey
1 tablespoon balsamic
    vinegar
1 teaspoon salt
pepper to taste
1/2 cup chopped toasted
    walnuts

Garnish
basil sprigs

Cucumber and Lobster Soup

Peel the cucumbers partially with a vegetable peeler and slice crosswise 1/2 inch thick. Toss with 2 teaspoons salt in a colander placed over a bowl. Let stand for 1 hour, reserving the juices that accumulate in the bowl.

Process the cucumbers with the reserved liquid in a blender until smooth. Strain through a fine sieve, pressing to extract all the liquid. Combine the liquid with the lime juice, nutmeg, salt and pepper in a bowl.

Beat the whipping cream in a chilled bowl until soft peaks form. Fold gently into the cucumber liquid. Chill, covered, for 2 hours.

Ladle the soup into serving bowls and top with the lobster meat. Garnish with chives or basil.

Serves Four

Ingredients
2 pounds unwaxed
    cucumbers
2 teaspoons salt
3 tablespoons lime juice
1/8 teaspoon nutmeg
salt and pepper to taste
1 cup whipping cream
cooked meat of 2 lobster
    tails, chopped

Garnish
fresh chives or basil

Melon and Red Onions with Feta and Walnuts

Ingredients
2 red onions, sliced ¼ inch
   thick
1 tablespoon vegetable oil
2 cantaloupes
1 honeydew melon
¼ cup chopped fresh mint
   leaves
1 tablespoon fresh lime
   juice
pepper to taste
½ cup crumbled feta
   cheese
¼ cup toasted pine nuts

Sauté the onions in the heated oil in a large skillet over medium heat just until tender. Cool the onions to room temperature.

Cut a slice from the top and bottom of each melon. Place each on end and remove the peel, cutting from top to bottom. Cut into halves, discarding the seeds. Cut 1 cantaloupe half and 1 honeydew half into 1-inch wedges. Arrange the wedges on a serving platter.

Cut the remaining melon into ¾-inch chunks. Combine with the mint, lime juice and pepper in a bowl and toss to mix well. Spoon over the melon wedges. Top with the onions, feta cheese and pine nuts. Chill until serving time. Toss to serve.

Serves Eight

Bear Lake Raspberry Mold

Ingredients
1 (3-ounce) package
   raspberry gelatin
1 cup boiling water
1 tablespoon lemon juice
2 cups fresh raspberries
1 envelope unflavored
   gelatin
½ cup warm water
1 cup heavy cream
½ cup sugar
1 cup sour cream
1 teaspoon vanilla extract

Dissolve the raspberry gelatin in the boiling water in a bowl. Add the lemon juice and raspberries. Pour into a 6-cup mold and chill until firm.

Soften the unflavored gelatin in the warm water in a small bowl. Heat the heavy cream with the sugar in a saucepan over low heat just until the sugar dissolves. Add the softened gelatin, stirring to dissolve completely. Stir in the sour cream and vanilla. Cool slightly. Spoon gradually over the congealed layer.

Chill the mold until firm. Unmold onto a serving plate.

Serves Six to Eight

The word is out that Jell-O and Utah are inseparable. During the recent 100-year anniversary of the rainbow-hued fruit-flavored staple of the 1950s, it was revealed that Salt Lake City leads the world in the consumption of America's best-selling prepared dessert. It is at its finest, however, filled with Utah's fresh raspberries.

Black Bean and Rice Salad

Bring the chicken broth and water to a boil in a large heavy saucepan. Add the long-grain and wild rice and bay leaves and return to a boil. Reduce the heat to low and cover. Simmer for 20 minutes or until the liquid is absorbed. Remove to a large bowl and fluff with a fork, discarding the bay leaves.

Add the beans, bell peppers, onion, cilantro, olive oil, orange juice, vinegar, cumin, chili powder, salt and pepper; mix well. Chill for up to 24 hours.

Line a serving plate with lettuce leaves. Mound the salad in the center and garnish with cilantro sprigs.

Serves Twelve

Ingredients
2 (14-ounce) cans reduced-
   sodium chicken broth
1/2 cup water
8 ounces uncooked long-
   grain rice
8 ounces uncooked wild
   rice
2 bay leaves
2 (15-ounce) cans black
   beans, drained, rinsed
2 red bell peppers, chopped
1 medium red onion,
   chopped
1 medium bunch cilantro,
   chopped
1/2 cup olive oil
3 tablespoons orange juice
2 tablespoons red wine
   vinegar
2 teaspoons ground cumin
1 teaspoon chili powder
salt and pepper to taste
lettuce leaves

Garnish
cilantro sprigs

Green Bean and Fennel Salad

Ingredients
1¹/₂ pounds fresh green
   beans, trimmed
1 to 1¹/₂ pounds fennel
   bulbs
1 head radicchio
¹/₂ cup plus 1 tablespoon
   olive oil
3 tablespoons balsamic
   vinegar
1¹/₂ cups coarsely grated
   Parmesan cheese
salt and freshly ground
   pepper to taste

Garnish
¹/₄ cup coarsely grated
   Parmesan cheese

Boil the green beans in water to cover in a large saucepan for 8 minutes or until tender-crisp. Drain and rinse under cold water; pat dry with a towel and place in a large bowl.

Trim the fennel and cut into quarters lengthwise. Slice lengthwise, discarding the cores. Add to the beans. Cut the radicchio into halves and slice lengthwise, discarding the core. Add to the beans. Chill for up to 24 hours if desired.

Drizzle first with the olive oil and then with the vinegar, tossing to coat well. Add the cheese, salt and pepper and toss gently.

Spoon into a serving bowl. Garnish with the cheese and serve immediately.

Serves Twelve

Summer

Both green beans and fennel are wonderful summer-into-autumn vegetables to be enjoyed in a variety of ways. All parts of the fennel plant, from the bulb to the feathery greenery, are edible if the rough or dry outer leaves are trimmed away. Fennel is sweeter and more delicate than anise, the licorice-flavored plant with which it is often confused. The base and stems of the fennel bulb sliced raw in salads give a refreshing crunch. It can also be sliced and sautéed or boiled and puréed.

Great Salt Lake Caesar Salad

For the dressing, process the garlic in a food processor until minced. Add the mayonnaise, anchovies with capers, Parmesan cheese, lemon juice, Worcestershire sauce and mustard; process until smooth. Spoon into a medium container with a lid. Chill until serving time.

For the croutons, sauté the garlic in the heated olive oil in a large heavy skillet over low heat for 8 minutes or until golden brown. Remove the garlic with a slotted spoon and discard. Add the bread cubes and cook for 15 minutes over low heat or until golden brown, stirring frequently. Remove from the skillet and cool to room temperature.

To prepare the salad, toss the lettuce with enough of the dressing to coat well. Add the Parmesan cheese and croutons and toss gently. Spoon onto chilled serving plates.

Serves Four

Caesar Dressing
3 cloves of garlic
3/4 cup mayonnaise or low-fat mayonnaise
3 canned rolled anchovy fillets with capers, drained
2 tablespoons grated Parmesan cheese
1 tablespoon lemon juice
1 teaspoon Worcestershire sauce
1 teaspoon Dijon mustard

Caesar Croutons
4 cloves of garlic, cut into halves
1/4 cup olive oil
4 cups (3/4-inch) bread cubes made from trimmed day-old bread

Salad
l large head romaine lettuce, chopped
1/3 cup grated Parmesan cheese

The Great Salt Lake is in the northeastern part of Utah's Basin and Range Region. It is the country's largest lake west of the Mississippi River, and it covers more than 1,700 square miles. True to its name, it is much saltier than any sea except the Dead Sea, because many rivers flow into it but none flow out. When the water evaporates, great salt deposits are left behind. The main reason to visit the Great Salt Lake is not for floating unsinkable in its salty waters, as people inevitably want to try, but to visit Antelope Island State Park, home to a wild buffalo herd and many other wonders of nature.

Cucina's Mediterranean Potato Salad

Potato Salad Dressing
1/2 cup olive oil
1/4 cup red wine vinegar
2 tablespoons chopped
    fresh parsley
1 teaspoon salt
1/2 teaspoon freshly ground
    pepper

Salad
3 pounds new potatoes
1 tablespoon salt
2 medium tomatoes,
    chopped
1/2 cup chopped red onion
1/2 cup kalamata olive
    halves
1 tablespoon capers
1 tablespoon minced garlic

For the dressing, whisk the olive oil, vinegar, parsley, salt and pepper in a small bowl until well mixed.

For the salad, cut the potatoes into 1-inch pieces. Cook with the salt in water to cover in a saucepan until tender; drain and cool.

Combine the tomatoes, onion, olives, capers and garlic in a medium bowl. Add the potatoes and dressing and mix gently. Chill for 1 hour or longer.

Serves Six to Eight

Cucina is a specialty food market and deli located in the historic Avenues district of Salt Lake City. Locals crowd into the bright European-style café every day to enjoy the outstanding food and ambiance created by Cucina's partners, Marguerite Henderson and Eileen McPartland. Their salads are always a favorite. Henderson says this one is perfect for picnics and tastes even better if you make it hours ahead of time.

Coleslaw

For the dressing, combine the mayonnaise, vinegar, sugar, celery seeds and salt in a bowl and mix well.

For the salad, combine the cabbage and green onions in a bowl. Add the desired amount of dressing and mix well. Chill for 2 hours to blend flavors.

Serves Six to Eight

Coleslaw Dressing
1 cup mayonnaise
2 tablespoons white wine vinegar
2 tablespoons sugar
2 teaspoons celery seeds
1 teaspoon salt

Coleslaw
6 cups chopped cabbage
1/4 cup chopped green onions and tops

Marinated Tomatoes

Combine the olive oil, vinegar, garlic, onion, parsley, basil, salt and pepper in a covered jar and shake to mix well.

Cut the tomatoes into 1/2-inch slices. Arrange in a large shallow dish. Pour the dressing over the slices.

Marinate the tomatoes in the refrigerator for several hours. Serve on lettuce leaves and garnish with basil sprigs.

Serves Four

Ingredients
1/3 cup olive oil
1/4 cup red wine vinegar
1/2 clove of garlic, crushed
2 tablespoons chopped onion
1 tablespoon chopped parsley
1 tablespoon chopped basil
salt and pepper to taste
3 large tomatoes
lettuce leaves

Garnish
basil sprigs

Classic Iceberg Side Salad

Ingredients
1 head iceberg lettuce
1 cup sliced hearts of palm
2 hard-cooked eggs,
    chopped
1 cup crumbled crisp-fried
    bacon
1/4 cup chopped chives
3/4 cup crumbled bleu
    cheese
1/2 teaspoon Worcestershire
    sauce
1/2 teaspoon salt
1/2 teaspoon pepper
1/3 cup red wine vinegar
1/4 cup vegetable oil

Garnish
cherry tomatoes

Reserve 4 large lettuce leaves and chop the remaining lettuce into bite-size pieces. Combine the chopped lettuce with the hearts of palm, eggs, bacon, chives, bleu cheese, Worcestershire sauce, salt and pepper in a large bowl. Drizzle with the vinegar and oil and toss to coat well.

Place the lettuce leaves on 4 chilled plates. Spoon the salad onto the lettuce leaves. Garnish with cherry tomatoes.

Serves Four to Eight

The Watchman at Sunset
Seen from Springdale, Zion National Park

Mesclun is a term that means a mix of young salad greens. It may include arugula, frisée, totsoi, mizuma, oak leaf, mâche, radicchio, and sorrel. Some produce sections label it "gourmet salad mix."

Grilled Vegetable Salad with Goat Cheese Croutons

Balsamic Vinaigrette
3 tablespoons balsamic
    vinegar
1 tablespoon minced red
    onion
1 tablespoon honey
1/2 cup olive oil
salt and freshly ground
    pepper to taste

Goat Cheese Croutons
8 (1/2-inch) slices French or
    Italian bread
olive oil
salt and freshly ground
    pepper to taste
8 (1/4-inch) slices goat
    cheese
1 tablespoon fresh thyme
    leaves

Salad
1 each medium red and
    yellow bell pepper
1 medium zucchini
1 medium yellow squash
1 baby Italian eggplant
1 stalk broccoli
4 new potatoes
olive oil
4 cups mesclun, or mixed
    red and green leaf
    lettuce

For the vinaigrette, combine the vinegar, onion and honey in a blender container and process until smooth. Add the olive oil gradually, processing constantly. Season with salt and pepper. Chill for up to 24 hours. Bring to room temperature before serving.

For the croutons, brush both sides of the bread with olive oil and sprinkle with salt and pepper. Place on a baking sheet. Toast at 350 degrees for 4 minutes or until light brown, turning once. Top each crouton with a slice of goat cheese and sprinkle with thyme, salt and pepper.

For the salad, prepare a charcoal or wood fire and let it burn down to embers or preheat the broiler. Cut the bell peppers in quarters lengthwise and discard the seeds. Slice the zucchini, yellow squash and eggplant lengthwise 1/4 inch thick. Blanch the broccoli and cut into florets with some stem attached. Boil the potatoes and slice 1/4 inch thick.

Brush the vegetables with olive oil. Grill for 2 1/2 minutes on each side or until tender-crisp and marked by the grill. Combine with 1/4 cup of the vinaigrette and mix well.

Combine the mesclun with 2 tablespoons of the vinaigrette and toss lightly. Spoon onto 4 plates and arrange the vegetables around the greens, distributing them evenly. Top each serving with 2 croutons.

Serves Four

*Find the freshest rosemary available to use in roasting
and grilling recipes. It will impart a delicious flavor and fill
the air with an irresistible aroma.*

Roasted Chicken Salad with Bell Pepper and Onion

For the vinaigrette, mix the mustard and vinegar in a medium bowl. Add the olive oil gradually, mixing until smooth. Stir in the orange peel and rosemary.

For the salad, combine the olive oil, vinegar, garlic, rosemary and red pepper in a medium bowl and mix well.

Cut the chicken into 1-inch pieces. Brush the chicken on all sides with the olive oil mixture; place in a large baking dish. Cut the bell peppers into 1/2-inch strips. Cut the onions into 1/2-inch slices. Combine the vegetables with the remaining olive oil mixture in a bowl and toss to mix well. Divide the mixture between 2 large baking sheets.

Roast the vegetables at 425 degrees for 40 minutes or until the edges are brown. Roast the chicken for 25 minutes or until cooked through.

Spoon the vegetables and chicken onto serving plates. Season with salt and pepper. Drizzle with the vinaigrette. Chill for up to 24 hours.

Serves Eight

Rosemary Vinaigrette
2 teaspoons Dijon mustard
2 teaspoons balsamic
  vinegar
1/4 cup olive oil
4 teaspoons grated orange
  peel
1 teaspoon fresh rosemary,
  or 1/2 teaspoon dried

Salad
2/3 cup olive oil
2/3 cup balsamic vinegar
6 cloves of garlic, minced
1/4 cup chopped fresh
  rosemary, or
  2 tablespoons dried
1/2 teaspoon crushed
  red pepper
4 pounds boneless skinless
  chicken breasts
3 large red bell peppers
2 large yellow bell peppers
3 large purple onions
salt and pepper to taste

Smoked Turkey Salad

Turkey Salad

1¼ pounds smoked turkey
    breast, chopped
1 cup chopped green
    onions
¾ cup chopped celery
⅓ cup low-fat mayonnaise
2 tablespoons chopped
    fresh thyme
salt and pepper to taste
2⅓ cups coarsely chopped
    pitted cherries
½ cup coarsely chopped
    toasted walnuts

*Thyme Vinaigrette and
Green Salad*

6 tablespoons olive oil
3 tablespoons white wine
    vinegar
1 tablespoon chopped fresh
    thyme
salt and pepper to taste
8 ounces mixed baby
    greens

For the turkey salad, combine the turkey, green onions, celery, mayonnaise and thyme in a medium bowl. Season with salt and pepper and mix well. Add the cherries and walnuts and mix gently.

For the vinaigrette, whisk the olive oil, vinegar and thyme in a small bowl until smooth. Season with salt and pepper.

Combine the vinaigrette with the greens in a large bowl and toss to mix well. Spoon onto serving plates. Spoon the turkey salad onto the top. Serve with warm wheat bread.

Serves Six

Moroni, Utah, is famous for raising turkeys—lots and lots of turkeys. Utah is also proud of the cherries that ripen in the early summer, when you can pick your own at cherry farms.

Asian Shrimp and Noodle Salad

Whisk the salad dressing, soy sauce, basil and ginger together in a large bowl. Add the shrimp and mix well. Marinate for 10 minutes.

Cook the pasta al dente using the package directions. Drain and rinse in cold water until cool. Add to the shrimp mixture with the cucumber; toss to coat well. Season with salt and pepper.

Spoon the salad onto serving plates. Garnish with the basil.

Serves Four

Ingredients
2/3 cup oil and vinegar
    salad dressing
1/4 cup reduced-sodium soy
    sauce
1/2 cup chopped fresh basil
2 tablespoons minced
    peeled ginger
1 pound cooked peeled
    shrimp
12 ounces uncooked
    vermicelli or thin
    spaghetti
2/3 cup juilienned English
    cucumber
salt and pepper to taste

Garnish
2 tablespoons chopped
    fresh basil

Julienne-cut vegetables make a difference in the presentation of a dish. The term julienned or julienne-cut refers to items cut into matchstick strips 2 or 3 inches long, as the cucumber, carrots, and bell pepper are in this recipe.

Ginger Peanut Pasta Salad

Ginger Vinaigrette
1/4 cup salad oil
2 teaspoons chili oil
1/4 cup rice wine vinegar
2 tablespoons soy sauce
2 tablespoons sugar
2 tablespoons grated fresh
   ginger

Salad
8 ounces uncooked tri-color
   corkscrew pasta
20 fresh peapods
1 medium cucumber,
   julienned
2 medium carrots,
   julienned
1 medium yellow bell
   pepper, julienned
1/2 cup sliced green onions
3/4 cup thinly sliced
   radishes
1/2 bunch fresh cilantro,
   chopped
1/3 cup chopped peanuts

For the vinaigrette, combine the salad oil, chili oil, vinegar, soy sauce, sugar and ginger in a covered jar; shake to mix well. Chill until serving time.

For the salad, cook the pasta using the package directions, adding the peapods during the last 30 seconds; drain and rinse.

Combine the cucumber, carrots, bell pepper, green onions and radishes in a large bowl. Add the pasta, peapods and cilantro and mix well. Chill in the refrigerator.

Toss the salad with the vinaigrette in a serving bowl 30 minutes before serving. Add the peanuts just before serving; toss to mix well.

Serves Six to Eight

Cilantro, one of the most popular herbs in Asian, Caribbean, and Latin American cooking, is actually the green leaf of the coriander plant; the spice coriander is the dried seeds. Although the two are often confused, their flavors are different and not interchangeable. Cilantro has a distinctive pungent flavor and people either like it a lot, or not at all! It is best used fresh, chopped and sprinkled on dishes after they are cooked.

Bleu Cheese Walnut Butter can be prepared up to two days in advance. Double it and use the leftovers in stuffed potatoes.

Steaks with Bleu Cheese Walnut Butter

For the butter, combine the butter, cheese, parsley and rosemary in a medium bowl and mix well. Stir in the walnuts, salt and pepper. Chill until needed; bring to room temperature before serving.

For the steaks, combine the rosemary, garlic, salt and pepper in a food processor and process to a coarse paste.

Pat the steaks dry. Rub 2 teaspoons of the garlic paste on each side of each steak; place in a large pan. Let stand, covered, at room temperature for 1 hour.

Grill the steaks for 5 minutes on each side for medium-rare. Remove to a serving platter; cut into 3 equal portions or cut into thick slices.

Place on serving plates and top each serving with the butter. Serve immediately with roasted new potatoes and a good Merlot.

Serves Six

Bleu Cheese Walnut Butter
$1/4$ cup butter, softened
6 ounces bleu cheese, crumbled
2 tablespoons chopped parsley
$3/4$ teaspoon dried rosemary, crumbled
$1/4$ cup chopped toasted walnuts
salt and pepper to taste

Steaks
1 tablespoon dried rosemary, crumbled
6 large cloves of garlic
1 teaspoon salt
$1^1/2$ teaspoons pepper
2 ($1^1/2$- to $1^3/4$-pound) boneless steaks, 1 inch thick

There are some basic tips that make a difference in grilling. Bring foods to room temperature before grilling. Cook only over super-hot coals covered with gray ash, which take about 30 to 45 minutes after lighting. Partially precook certain foods, such as chicken on the bone, spareribs, or very thick cuts of meat, before grilling meat to prevent drying out and assure that the meat is thoroughly cooked.

Pulled Pork is a special treat when Utah's peaches are in season. Owners of peach orchards in Pleasant Grove make it on canning day—a dawn to dusk event.

Pulled Pork with Peaches

Ingredients

1 (5-pound) boneless pork roast

4 cups sliced peeled peaches

²/₃ cup catsup

²/₃ cup vinegar

¹/₄ cup soy sauce

1 cup packed brown sugar

2 tablespoons minced garlic

2 tablespoons grated fresh ginger

Place the pork roast in a slow cooker. Cook on Low for 5 hours. Remove the roast and shred with 2 forks. Discard the cooking liquids and return the roast to the slow cooker.

Combine the peaches, catsup, vinegar, soy sauce, brown sugar, garlic and ginger in a blender container. Process until smooth. Mix with the pork. Cook for 1 to 2 hours longer.

Serve on buns. Add coleslaw for a Southern touch.

Serves Twelve

Summer

Chicken in Triple-Mustard Marinade

Whisk together the Dijon mustard, hot mustard, whole-grain mustard, vinegar, oil and apple juice in a medium bowl. Add the shallots and tarragon. Store in the refrigerator for up to 1 week.

Combine the marinade with the chicken in a shallow dish. Marinate in the refrigerator for 4 to 6 hours; drain.

Grill the chicken until cooked through and juices run clear when the chicken is pierced.

Serves Six

Ingredients
1/4 cup Dijon mustard
1/4 cup hot mustard
1/4 cup whole-grain
  mustard
1/4 cup white vinegar
1/4 cup salad oil
1/2 cup apple juice
shallots and tarragon
  (optional)
2 pounds chicken

Grilled Utah fruit is absolutely wonderful with meats and fish. Try firm ripe peach or nectarine halves or wedges of juicy ripe melon or fresh pineapple. Brush the fruit with your favorite oil-based marinade and place on the grill for the last 10 minutes of the meat's grilling time, turning once. Sprinkle it with chopped basil, cilantro, or other herbs to complement the meat.

Green River Chicken Stir-Fry

Stir-Fry Marinade
2 teaspoons oyster sauce
1 1/2 teaspoons white wine
1 teaspoon light soy sauce
1 teaspoon sesame oil
3/4 teaspoon grated fresh
    ginger
2 teaspoons cornstarch
3/4 teaspoon sugar
1/2 teaspoon salt
white pepper to taste

Chicken Stir-Fry
8 ounces boneless skinless
    chicken breasts
1/2 cup snow peas
4 scallions
1 tablespoon peanut oil
3 tablespoons peanut oil
1/4 teaspoon salt
1 1/2 cups (1-inch pieces)
    honeydew melon
1 1/2 cups (1-inch pieces)
    cantaloupe
2 tablespoons peanut oil
1 tablespoon minced garlic

Garnish
1/3 cup chopped cashews

For the marinade, combine the oyster sauce, wine, soy sauce, sesame oil, ginger, cornstarch, sugar, salt and white pepper in a bowl and mix well.

For the stir-fry, pound the chicken with a meat mallet. Cut diagonally across the grain into 1/2-inch slices. Add to the marinade and marinate in the refrigerator for 2 hours or longer.

Slice the snow peas diagonally into 1/2-inch pieces, removing the strings. Cut the white portions of the scallions into 1/2-inch pieces.

Heat a wok over high heat for 45 seconds. Add 1 tablespoon of the peanut oil and swirl to coat evenly. Add the salt and heat until a wisp of white smoke appears. Add the snow peas and scallions. Stir-fry for 1 minute or until the snow peas are bright green. Add the honeydew and cantaloupe. Stir-fry for 1 minute or until heated through. Remove with a slotted spoon and wipe the wok with a paper towel.

Reheat the wok, add 2 tablespoons peanut oil and heat until a wisp of smoke appears. Add the garlic and stir-fry for 30 seconds or until light brown. Add the chicken and cook for 1 minute without stirring. Turn the chicken and cook for 30 to 60 seconds or until cooked through.

Return the melon and vegetables to the wok. Cook for 30 to 60 seconds or until heated through. Serve immediately with or over rice. Garnish with the cashews.

Serves Four to Six

Crystal Creek Salmon

Rinse the salmon and place on a foil-lined baking sheet. Cut the onion, orange and lemon into $1/3$-inch slices. Squeeze the juice from the orange and lemon over the salmon; place the squeezed slices and onion slices over the fish. Top with the dill. Pull up the sides of the foil and add the water. Cover with foil and seal the edges securely.

To grill the salmon, grill over high heat for 15 to 20 minutes or until cooked through but not dry. To oven-poach the salmon, bake at 500 degrees for 5 to 8 minutes or until cooked through.

Serves Four

Ingredients
2 pounds salmon fillets
1 small yellow onion
1 orange
1 lemon
1 bunch fresh dill
$1/2$ cup water or wine

Shrimp Bob-Style

Cook the pasta using the package directions. Remove from the heat and add the shrimp to the pasta. Set aside.

Sauté the garlic in the melted butter in a skillet until light brown. Drain the pasta and shrimp and combine with the garlic and butter in a bowl and toss lightly.

Add the basil, tomatoes and salt; toss to mix well. Top with the cheese. Serve with a salad and bread.

Serves Two or Three

Ingredients
9 ounces uncooked linguine
    or angel hair pasta
20 medium shrimp, peeled
    with tails intact, cooked
1 tablespoon chopped
    garlic
$1/4$ cup butter
3 tablespoons chopped
    fresh basil
2 medium tomatoes,
    seeded, chopped
salt to taste
$1/3$ to $1/2$ cup grated
    Parmesan cheese

Though most fly fishermen are advocates of catch-and-release, Utah's fishermen do consume their fair share of local fish, including trout, striped bass, walleyes, bluegills, whitefish, and Bonneville cisco.

Café Diablo
Pumpkin Seed-Crusted Trout

Trout
4 (6- to 8-ounce) trout fillets
$^{1}/_{2}$ cup flour
$^{1}/_{2}$ cup egg wash
1 cup unsalted green
    pumpkin seeds, slightly
    crushed
2 tablespoons olive oil

Lime Butter Sauce
$^{1}/_{2}$ cup white wine
juice of 2 limes
1 ounce chopped cilantro
6 tablespoons butter
salt to taste

For the trout, coat the meaty side of the trout fillets with flour. Dip in the egg wash and then in the pumpkin seeds. Heat the olive oil in a 10-inch sauté pan and add the fillets seed side down. Sauté over medium heat for 5 minutes or until the seeds are brown. Turn the trout. Sauté for 10 minutes longer. Bake at 325 degrees for 10 minutes. Remove to serving plates.

For the sauce, add the wine and lime juice to the sauté pan. Bring to a boil over high heat and reduce the heat. Simmer for 2 minutes. Add the cilantro, butter and salt. Cook over high heat until thickened and creamy, whisking to mix well. Spoon over the fish.

Serves Four

Gary and Jane Pankow, chef and pastry chef respectively, are the proud owners of Café Diablo in Torrey, near Capitol Reef National Park. Though their restaurant would stand out anywhere in the country, it is an especially welcome beacon in this tiny town. Home to numerous artists, writers, and lovers of Utah's nearby wilderness, the Torrey area also boasts some great fishing, but only for private consumption. Pankow's trout are farm-raised in nearby waters and are pleasingly plump and delicious in this original recipe that draws people from near and far.

Carrots Provençal

Cut the carrots diagonally into ¹/₂-inch pieces. Heat the olive oil in a large skillet over medium-high heat. Add the carrots and stir to coat well. Reduce the heat to medium, cover, and braise for 20 minutes, stirring frequently.

Add the garlic and salt. Cook over low heat for 15 minutes longer or until the carrots are almost caramelized and the garlic is tender. Sprinkle with the olives and adjust the seasoning. Serve hot or at room temperature.

Serves Four or Five

Corn with Shallot Thyme Butter

For the butter, sauté the shallots and garlic in 2 tablespoons of the butter in a small heavy skillet over medium heat for 4 minutes or until golden brown. Cool to room temperature.

Blend the remaining 6 tablespoons butter with the thyme in a small bowl. Add the shallot mixture and mix well. Season with salt and pepper. Chill for up to 2 days at this point; bring to room temperature before serving.

To grill the corn, brush the ears with olive oil. Grill away from the direct heat on a medium-high grill for 10 minutes or until the corn is tender and beginning to brown in a few places, turning frequently. To boil the corn, cook in a large saucepan of salted water for 6 minutes or until tender; drain. Serve with the shallot thyme butter.

Serves Six

Ingredients
1 pound carrots, peeled
1 tablespoon olive oil
6 large cloves of garlic, cut into halves
salt to taste
¹/₄ cup chopped black olives

Shallot Thyme Butter
²/₃ cup chopped shallots
3 cloves of garlic, minced
8 tablespoons butter, softened
2 tablespoons chopped fresh thyme
salt and pepper to taste

Corn
6 to 9 ears of fresh corn, husked
olive oil or salt

Goat Cheese and Thyme Potato Cake

Ingredients
1¹/₂ pounds small red
   potatoes
salt to taste
4 ounces Montrachet or
   other goat cheese
6 tablespoons butter,
   softened
¹/₂ cup sour cream
2 eggs
1 teaspoon fresh thyme
   leaves

Oil or butter a 9x9-inch baking pan and line with an 8x14-inch piece of baking parchment, allowing the ends of the paper to overhang the pan. Oil the portion of the parchment in the pan.

Slice the potatoes ¹/₄ inch thick. Cook in boiling salted water to cover in a saucepan for 8 minutes or until tender but still firm. Drain in a colander and cool for 15 minutes.

Grate a firm aged goat cheese, or force a softer cheese through a sieve. Whisk the butter and sour cream in a large bowl until smooth. Whisk in the goat cheese and eggs. Add the potatoes and toss lightly.

Spoon the mixture into the prepared pan; smooth with a spatula. Sprinkle with the thyme. Bake at 375 degrees on the center oven rack for 35 minutes or until the top is golden brown. Cool in the pan on a wire rack. Refrigerate, covered, for up to 2 days at this point if desired.

Lift the potato cake from the pan using the overhanging parchment and remove to a cutting board. Cut into squares and discard the parchment. Serve at room temperature.

Serves Six

Skewers of Summer Squash

For the marinade, combine the pineapple juice, soy sauce, lemon juice, vinegar, honey, canola oil, ginger and garlic in a glass bowl and whisk until well mixed.

For the skewers, slice the zucchini and summer squash crosswise 1/2 inch thick. Place in the marinade and toss to coat well. Marinate at room temperature for 1 hour. Discard the stems of small mushrooms and leave whole, or cut large mushrooms into halves. Add to the marinade and marinate for 30 minutes longer.

Soak 6 wooden skewers in water for 30 minutes. Preheat a charcoal grill or gas grill to medium-high, allowing 15 to 20 minutes for charcoal and 10 minutes for gas.

Drain the vegetables, reserving the marinade. Thread the vegetables alternately onto the skewers; brush with olive oil. Grill for 20 minutes or until fork tender, turning every 5 minutes.

Bring the reserved marinade to a boil. Spoon into small bowls to use as dipping sauce for the skewers.

Serves Six

Pineapple Ginger Marinade
1/2 cup unsweetened
   pineapple juice
2 tablespoons reduced-
   sodium soy sauce
2 tablespoons fresh lemon
   juice
1 tablespoon white wine
   vinegar
1 tablespoon honey
1 tablespoon canola oil
1 tablespoon grated fresh
   ginger
2 cloves of garlic, minced

Squash Skewers
12 ounces (3 small)
   zucchini
1 pound (3 medium)
   yellow crookneck squash
8 ounces mushrooms
1 teaspoon olive oil

Vegetable Frittata

Ingredients
12 large eggs
1½ cups half-and-half
½ teaspoon salt
½ teaspoon pepper
1 small red onion, thinly
    sliced
½ red bell pepper, chopped
1 small zucchini, chopped
2 tablespoons butter
½ cup shredded Cheddar
    cheese
2 tablespoons chopped
    fresh basil

Beat the eggs with the half-and-half in a medium bowl until frothy. Beat in the salt and pepper.

Sauté the onion, bell pepper and zucchini in the butter in an ovenproof nonstick 10-inch skillet until tender. Add the egg mixture. Cook over medium heat for 2 minutes. Sprinkle with the cheese and basil.

Bake at 375 degrees on the center oven rack for 10 minutes or until the eggs are puffed and firm in the center. Let stand for several minutes. Cut into wedges and serve immediately.

Serves Eight

Pistachio and Currant Bulgur

Ingredients
3 cups uncooked bulgur
2¼ cups chicken broth
1 cup dried currants
9 tablespoons lemon juice
¾ cup olive oil
½ teaspoon cinnamon
salt and pepper to taste
1½ cups pistachios
¾ cup chopped scallions

Add the bulgur to the boiling chicken broth in a saucepan. Cook for 10 to 15 minutes or until the liquid is absorbed, stirring occasionally. Stir in the currants.

Combine the lemon juice, olive oil, cinnamon, salt and pepper in a bowl. Add the bulgur, pistachios and scallions and mix well. Serve at room temperature.

Serves Eight

Moon over Delicate Arch
Arches National Park

Cook polenta in a deep saucepan over low heat to avoid hot spatters and stir it with a wooden spoon or large whisk. Store leftovers well wrapped in the refrigerator and serve them later, sliced, brushed with olive oil, and browned under the broiler or in a skillet with olive oil or butter.

Grilled Parmesan Polenta Squares

Ingredients
1 cup yellow cornmeal
3 cups low-sodium chicken
    broth
1 cup grated Parmesan
    cheese
salt and pepper to taste
olive oil

Whisk the cornmeal gradually into the boiling chicken broth in a heavy medium saucepan over medium-high heat. Reduce the heat to medium-low and cook for 5 minutes or until very thick, whisking constantly. Remove from the heat.

Whisk in half the cheese and season with salt and pepper. Pour into a greased 8x8-inch dish and smooth the top. Chill, covered, for 30 minutes to 12 hours.

Cut the polenta into squares; brush with olive oil. Arrange oiled side down on foil and brush with olive oil. Place the foil on a preheated grill. Grill for 3 minutes on each side or until heated through. Remove to a platter. Sprinkle with the remaining cheese.

Serves Six to Eight

Once known as an Italian peasant dish, polenta has become a favorite on menus in Utah and all over the country. It can be found in prepared form in many supermarkets, or it can be cooked in chicken broth, milk, water, or a combination of these. It can be served like potatoes as a side dish or combined with a variety of ingredients, from chicken to sausage, as a main dish. Utah cheeses of all kinds make it thick and creamy.

The main ingredient in risotto is arborio rice, a short-grain starchy rice prized for its ability to absorb liquid and create a rich, creamy consistency in any of its many versions, combining savory liquids and fresh ingredients.

Risotto Giardino

Heat the butter and olive oil in a medium saucepan over medium-low heat. Add the onion and cook until light brown. Add the rice. Cook for 5 minutes or until the liquid is absorbed, stirring constantly.

Heat the chicken broth in a saucepan. Add ¼ cup at a time to the rice, cooking until the broth is absorbed after each addition and stirring constantly.

Add the wine, tomatoes, artichokes, carrots, zucchini and green beans. Cook until the rice is al dente and the liquid is absorbed. Stir in the cheese, salt and pepper.

Serves Four

Ingredients
2 tablespoons butter
1 tablespoon olive oil
¾ cup chopped onion
1 cup uncooked arborio rice
3 cups chicken stock
¼ cup dry white wine
¾ cup chopped fresh tomatoes
1 cup small unmarinated artichokes
½ cup julienned carrots, blanched
½ cup julienned zucchini
½ cup fresh green beans, blanched
¼ cup grated Parmesan cheese
salt and pepper to taste

Summer

In summer, Utahns take advantage of such additions to risotto as fresh tomatoes, sweet peas, fresh corn, squash, and bell peppers—anything and everything that looks good in their gardens and markets. When risotto calls for grated Parmesan, seek out the best imported Italian cheese that can be found. Buy it in chunks rather than grated, as grated cheese loses quality through exposure to air.

Blueberry French Toast

Ingredients
1 (8-ounce) loaf French
   bread
4 eggs
1/2 cup milk
1/4 teaspoon baking powder
1 teaspoon vanilla extract
4 1/2 cups fresh or partially
   thawed frozen
   blueberries
1/2 cup sugar
1 tablespoon (heaping)
   cornstarch
1 teaspoon cinnamon
2 tablespoons melted butter

Garnish
confectioners' sugar

Slice the bread diagonally into 10 to 14 slices 3/4 inch thick. Arrange in a single layer in a 9x13-inch dish.

Whisk the eggs, milk, baking powder and vanilla in a medium bowl until smooth. Pour gradually over the bread, turning to coat completely. Chill, covered with plastic wrap, for 8 hours or longer.

Combine the blueberries, sugar, cornstarch and cinnamon in a bowl and mix well. Spread evenly in a buttered 9x13-inch baking dish. Place the bread wettest side down over the blueberries. Brush with the melted butter.

Bake at 450 degrees for 20 to 25 minutes or until golden brown. Garnish with confectioners' sugar.

Serves Six to Eight

Banana Oat Bran Pancakes

Mix the oat bran, flour, baking soda and sugar in a medium bowl. Stir in the banana, yogurt and vanilla.

Beat the egg whites in a mixer bowl until soft peaks form. Fold $1/3$ of the mixture into the banana mixture. Fold in the remaining egg whites with the melted butter.

Heat a greased griddle or skillet to 375 degrees. Spoon the batter by $1/4$ cupfuls onto the griddle. Bake for 1 minute on each side or until golden brown.

Garnish with chopped pecans. Serve with warm syrup or sliced bananas and summer berries.

Serves Eight

Ingredients
1 cup oat bran
1 cup flour
2 teaspoons baking soda
1 tablespoon sugar
$1/2$ cup mashed ripe banana
$1^1/2$ cups plain yogurt
2 teaspoons vanilla extract
4 egg whites
2 tablespoons melted butter

Garnish
chopped pecans

Strawberry Bread

Ingredients
3 cups flour
2 cups sugar
1 teaspoon baking soda
1/2 teaspoon cinnamon
1 teaspoon salt
4 eggs
1 1/4 cups vegetable oil
2 cups sliced fresh
   strawberries

Mix the flour, sugar, baking soda, cinnamon and salt in a large bowl. Add the eggs, oil and strawberries and mix just until moistened.

Spoon into 2 greased and floured loaf pans. Bake at 350 degrees for 1 hour and 10 minutes. Cool in the pans for several minutes; remove to wire racks to cool completely.

Makes Two Loaves

Onion and Rosemary Bread

Ingredients
1 envelope fast-rising dry
   yeast
1 tablespoon sugar
1 1/2 cups lukewarm water
4 cups flour
2 teaspoons salt
1/2 cup chopped onion
vegetable oil
1 1/2 tablespoons fresh
   rosemary leaves
salt

Dissolve the yeast and sugar in the lukewarm water in a large bowl; stir to mix well. Add the flour, 2 teaspoons salt and onion; mix well. Knead on a floured surface until smooth and elastic.

Place the dough in a greased bowl, turning to coat the surface. Let rise until doubled in bulk. Punch down dough. Shape into a round 12-inch loaf on a greased baking sheet. Brush the top with oil. Let rise until doubled in bulk.

Sprinkle the top with the rosemary and additional salt. Bake at 400 degrees for 30 to 35 minutes or until the loaf is golden brown and sounds hollow when tapped. Serve hot.

Serves Eight

Fresh Apricot Turnovers

Combine the apricots, lemon juice, lemon zest, sugar, 1 tablespoon water, nutmeg and salt in a heavy saucepan. Cook over medium heat for 25 minutes or until thickened, stirring occasionally. Cool to room temperature.

Cut the pastry into 4- to 5-inch squares. Beat the egg with 1 tablespoon water. Spoon 2 to 3 tablespoons of the apricot mixture into the center of each square and moisten the corners with the egg mixture. Fold the pastry over diagonally to form a triangle and press to seal.

Place on a baking sheet. Brush with the egg mixture and sprinkle with additional sugar. Bake at 400 degrees for 20 to 25 minutes or until golden brown. Serve with vanilla ice cream.

Serves Six

Ingredients
1 pound fresh apricots, sliced
1 tablespoon lemon juice
grated zest of 1 lemon
3/4 cup sugar
1 tablespoon water
1/4 teaspoon nutmeg
salt to taste
pie pastry or puff pastry
1 egg
1 tablespoon water
sugar

Replace the liqueur in this trifle with a fruit syrup if you prefer.

Berry Season Trifle

Custard
1/2 cup milk
1/3 cup sugar
2 large eggs
1 egg yolk
1/4 cup cornstarch
2 cups milk
3 tablespoons sugar
1 tablespoon butter
grated zest of 1 lemon
2 teaspoons vanilla extract
2 tablespoons orange or
    peach liqueur, or sweet
    sherry

Trifle
1 (16-ounce) pound cake or
    sponge cake
orange or peach liqueur, or
    sweet sherry
fresh summer berries

Lemon Whipped Cream
2 cups whipping cream
1 tablespoon grated lemon
    zest
sugar to taste

Garnish
fresh summer berries
mint leaves

For the custard, combine 1/2 cup milk, 1/3 cup sugar, the eggs, egg yolk and cornstarch in a bowl and whisk until smooth. Combine 2 cups milk and 3 tablespoons sugar in a small heavy saucepan and bring almost to a boil over medium heat. Add gradually to the custard mixture, whisking constantly. Return to the saucepan and bring to a boil, whisking constantly. Cook until thickened and smooth, whisking constantly. Remove from the heat and whisk in the butter, lemon zest, vanilla and liqueur. Cool to room temperature.

To assemble the trifle, cut the cake into cubes or fingers. Sprinkle a layer of the cake in a trifle bowl. Drizzle with liqueur. Add a layer of custard and then berries, spreading each to the side of the bowl. Repeat the layers until all ingredients are used, ending with the custard. Chill, covered with plastic wrap, for 4 hours or longer.

For the whipped cream, combine the whipping cream and lemon zest in a small bowl and mix well. Chill, covered, for 24 hours.

Beat the whipping cream mixture in a mixer bowl until frothy. Add sugar to taste gradually, beating constantly until soft peaks form. Spread or pipe over the top of the trifle.

Garnish with additional berries and mint leaves.

Serves Six to Eight

Pastry chef Terry Gross of Salt Lake City notes, "This dessert is always a showstopper. It's a bit of a production but worth it! As for the fresh berries, I recommend raspberries, blueberries, and strawberries, in combination or all of one. Strawberries are my least favorite for this dessert, because they are a little juicier than the rest and tend to bleed into the trifle too much."

Cherry Cobbler

For the filling, combine the cherries, sugar, cornstarch, lemon juice, lemon peel, cinnamon and nutmeg in a bowl and mix well. Spoon into a buttered 9-inch baking dish. Dot with the butter.

For the pastry, mix the flour, 1/4 cup sugar, baking powder and salt in a bowl. Cut in the chilled butter with a pastry blender until the mixture has the texture of coarse cornmeal. Stir in the whipping cream to form a soft dough.

Roll the dough to a 6x6-inch square on a lightly floured surface. Cut into 2-inch squares or desired shapes with a 2-inch cutter. Arrange over the cherry filling. Brush with the melted butter and sprinkle with 2 tablespoons sugar. Bake at 400 degrees for 30 minutes or until the pastry is puffed and golden brown. Cool slightly.

For the whipped cream, mix the sour cream and brown sugar in a large bowl until the sugar dissolves. Add the whipping cream and rum. Beat until soft peaks form. Spoon onto the cobbler and serve immediately or serve with Old-Fashioned Ice Cream (page 109).

Substitute one 20-ounce package of frozen pitted cherries when fresh cherries are not available.

Serves Six

Filling
4 cups pitted tart cherries
3/4 cup sugar
2 tablespoons cornstarch
1 tablespoon fresh lemon juice
1 1/2 teaspoons grated lemon peel
1/2 teaspoon cinnamon
1/4 teaspoon nutmeg
3 tablespoons chilled butter, chopped

Cobbler Pastry
1/2 cup flour
1/4 cup sugar
1 1/2 teaspoons baking powder
1/2 teaspoon salt
2 tablespoons chilled butter, chopped
1/2 cup whipping cream
1 tablespoon melted butter
2 tablespoons sugar

Rum Whipped Cream
1/2 cup sour cream
1/4 cup packed brown sugar
1 cup whipping cream, chilled
2 tablespoons dark rum (optional)

Life is just a bowl of cherries in Utah's orchards. Utah is the nation's second-largest grower of tart cherries and fifth-largest grower of sweet cherries. Chefs especially prize the juicy Bing cherries.

Frozen Nectarine Mousse with Raspberries

Ingredients
2¹/₂ cups chopped
   nectarines
¹/₄ cup sugar
1 tablespoon lemon juice
¹/₄ cup water
¹/₂ cup plain yogurt
5 large egg yolks
¹/₄ cup sugar
5 large egg whites, at room
   temperature
2 tablespoons sugar
sliced nectarines
1 tablespoon lemon juice
fresh raspberries

Combine the chopped nectarines, ¹/₄ cup sugar, 1 tablespoon lemon juice and water in a heavy saucepan. Bring to a boil and reduce the heat, stirring constantly. Simmer for 10 to 12 minutes or until the nectarines are tender and the liquid is reduced to about 2 tablespoons. Spoon into a large bowl and cool. Stir in the yogurt.

Combine the egg yolks and ¹/₄ cup sugar in a metal bowl. Place over a saucepan of simmering water and cook for 3 to 5 minutes or until thick and light yellow, beating at high speed. Stir into the nectarine mixture.

Beat the egg whites in a mixer bowl until soft peaks form. Add 2 tablespoons sugar gradually, beating constantly until stiff peaks form. Stir ¹/₄ of the egg whites into the nectarine mixture. Fold in the remaining egg whites.

Spoon the mixture into a 5¹/₂-cup loaf pan lined with lightly oiled plastic wrap; cover with plastic wrap. Freeze for 8 to 48 hours.

Mix the nectarine slices with 1 tablespoon lemon juice in a bowl. Chill, covered, until serving time.

Dip the loaf pan into a bowl of warm water and invert onto a serving platter, discarding the plastic wrap. Drain the nectarine slices and arrange on top of the mousse. Sprinkle with the raspberries.

Serves Six

Old-Fashioned Ice Cream

For the ice cream, mix the sugar, sweetened condensed milk, whipping cream and vanilla in a bowl and mix well. Pour into an ice cream freezer container. Add milk to the fill line. Freeze using the freezer manufacturer's directions.

To add options, process the fruit with sugar to taste in a blender. Add to the sweetened condensed milk mixture and proceed as above.

Serves Twelve

Ingredients
1 cup sugar
2 (14-ounce) cans
   sweetened condensed
   milk
2 pints whipping cream
2 tablespoons vanilla
   extract
1/2 gallon whole milk

Options
1 pint fresh strawberries
1 pint fresh raspberries
1 pint fresh peaches, sliced
sugar to taste

Summer

In Utah, it seems we all scream for ice cream. In fact, we're the most appreciative ice cream consumers in America. At last count, we were up to 8.4 gallons per person, per year. We also rank nationally among the country's largest consumers of candy. We eat a total of more than 38 million pounds of every kind of candy, from chocolates to gummy bears, every year. Some say it's because Mormons, a group that constitutes a large percentage of the population, don't drink alcohol. Or, maybe it's just the altitude.

If you don't have tartlet pans, make the shortcake in an 8-inch cake pan and cut it into wedges to serve. The cakes and berry sauce can be made a day in advance. Store the cakes at room temperature and chill the sauce.

Peach Melba Shortcakes

Shortcakes
1/2 cup unsalted butter, softened
1/2 cup sugar
2 large eggs
1 teaspoon vanilla extract
1 1/4 cups cake flour
1 teaspoon baking powder
1/2 teaspoon baking soda
1/4 teaspoon salt
1/2 cup buttermilk
confectioners' sugar

Peach and Raspberry Filling and Raspberry Purée
4 large peaches, peeled, sliced
1/2 pint fresh raspberries
6 tablespoons sugar
1 (10-ounce) package frozen raspberries in syrup

Vanilla Whipped Cream
1 1/2 cups whipping cream, chilled
2 teaspoons vanilla extract
2 tablespoons sugar

For the shortcakes, brush six 4-inch tartlet pans with 1 1/8-inch sides and removable bottoms with melted butter. Place on a baking sheet. Cream the butter and sugar in a large mixer bowl until light and fluffy. Beat in the eggs 1 at a time. Beat in the vanilla. Sift the flour, baking powder, baking soda and salt over the mixture; mix lightly. Add the buttermilk and mix until moistened. Spoon into the prepared tartlet pans.

Bake at 350 degrees for 25 minutes or until a tester inserted into the center comes out clean. Cool in the pans on a wire rack for 5 minutes. Push up the bottoms of the pans to release the shortcakes. Cool on a wire rack. Cut into halves horizontally with a serrated knife. Sift confectioners' sugar lightly over the shortcake tops.

For the filling, combine the peaches, fresh raspberries and sugar in a medium bowl and toss to mix well. Let stand for 30 minutes or until juices form. For the purée, process the thawed frozen raspberries with their syrup in a food processor and strain.

For the whipped cream, beat the whipping cream with the vanilla and sugar in a medium bowl until soft peaks form.

To assemble the shortcakes, place the cake bottoms on individual serving plates. Top each with the peach mixture. Spoon whipped cream over the peaches. Replace the cake tops and spoon the raspberry purée around the cakes.

Serves Six

Plump, juicy, and ripe, with an alluring perfume, a soft rounded shape, velvety skin, and a blush of color—Utah's peaches are basically irresistible. Late summer varieties include silky-textured Elbertas, Red Havens, and Red Globes.

Chocolate-Covered Strawberries with Grand Marnier

Fill a syringe with the Grand Marnier and inject it into the strawberries. Melt the chocolate chips with the canola oil in a double boiler, stirring to blend well. Pat the strawberries dry and dip into the chocolate, coating evenly. Place on parchment and chill for 30 minutes.

Serves Two

Ingredients
2 tablespoons Grand Marnier
8 large strawberries
16 ounces chocolate chips
2 tablespoons canola oil

Brownies with Chocolate-Covered Raisins

Melt the semisweet and unsweetened chocolate with the butter in a saucepan over low heat, stirring to blend well. Cool completely.

Beat the sugar and eggs in a mixer bowl for 3 minutes or until thick and pale yellow. Add the melted chocolate and vanilla and mix well.

Mix the flour, baking powder and salt together. Add to the chocolate mixture and mix well. Stir in the raisins.

Spoon into a buttered 8x8-inch baking pan. Bake at 350 degrees for 30 minutes or until a tester inserted into the center comes out with a few moist crumbs, and the top cracks. Cool in the pan on a wire rack. Cut into squares.

Serves Twelve

Ingredients
6 ounces semisweet chocolate, chopped
1 ounce unsweetened chocolate, chopped
3/4 cup butter
3/4 cup sugar
2 large eggs
1 teaspoon vanilla extract
2/3 cup flour
3/4 teaspoon baking powder
1/4 teaspoon salt
1 cup chocolate-covered raisins

Serve with a bowl of freshly sliced Utah peaches.

Brown Sugar Shortbread Cookies

Ingredients
6 tablespoons butter, cut
    into 8 pieces
1/4 cup packed brown sugar
3/4 teaspoon vanilla extract
3/4 cup flour
1 tablespoon cornstarch
1/4 cup slivered almonds

Place a 9-inch metal pie pan in the freezer to chill.

Combine the butter, brown sugar and vanilla in a food processor and process for 20 seconds or until smooth. Add the flour and cornstarch. Pulse until the mixture forms a dough.

Press the dough evenly over the bottom of the chilled pie pan. Sprinkle with the almonds and press lightly into the dough. Place in the freezer for 5 minutes or until chilled.

Bake at 375 degrees for 22 minutes or until the edges are golden brown. Cool for several minutes. Cut warm shortbread into 8 wedges. Cool in the pan on a wire rack.

Serves Eight

The Best-Ever Lemonade

Scrub the lemons well and cut into halves. Place in a heat-resistant 2-quart pitcher. Add the sugar.

Bring the water to a boil in a saucepan. Pour it over the lemons, stirring to dissolve the sugar. Cool for 30 minutes. Squeeze the juice from the lemons into the pitcher and discard the lemons. Chill until serving time.

Serve over ice in tall glasses. Garnish with mint. Add a dash of grenadine for pink lemonade.

Serves Eight

Ingredients
6 juicy lemons
1 cup sugar
6 cups water

Garnish
mint sprigs

Raspberry Delight Slush

Boil the water and sugar in a saucepan for 3 minutes. Cool to room temperature. Add the lemon juice, orange juice, undrained pineapple and raspberries.

Pour into a freezer container. Freeze until firm. Let stand at room temperature until soft enough to scoop into a punch bowl or individual glasses. Add the soda to the punch bowl or glasses.

Serves Sixteen

Ingredients
3 cups water
2 cups sugar
juice of 1 lemon
2 cups orange juice
1 (20-ounce) can crushed
   pineapple
2 (10-ounce) packages
   frozen raspberries in
   syrup
1 (2-liter) bottle of
   lemon/lime soda, or
   1 large bottle of
   Champagne

The smell of fresh-crushed mint is the smell of summer in Utah. The most common types of mint found in local gardens and growing wild on mountain trails are peppermint and spearmint, which are generally interchangeable, although peppermint is stronger. Garden shops also provide mint varieties with subtle flavor variations, such as pineapple mint and chocolate mint. Enjoy minty pleasures in iced tea, lemonade, or rum with cola; steamed with fresh peas; chopped over couscous, basmati, or jasmine rice; over fresh tomatoes; or with garlic and a drizzle of oil as a topping for roasted new potatoes.

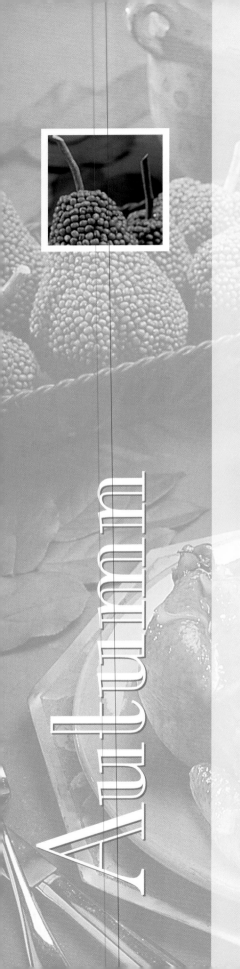

Autumn

Autumn in Utah tantalizes all the senses. As it eases us into a pattern of increasingly shorter days capped with brilliant sunsets, it transforms both desert and mountain landscapes. Oaks, cottonwoods, aspens, and maples in the canyons burst into every shade of red and yellow. Trees in the lower valleys soon join in the riot of color. In the desert, dusty sage contrasts with bright yellow rabbit brush.

Walking through Salt Lake's Avenues district, you're likely to smell the hint of wood smoke from chimneys atop the area's historic homes. Sunset over the coral-pink hoodoos of Bryce Canyon can be a chilly experience this time of year, but golfers are still wearing cotton shirts on the links in St. George.

Some years, Utah's garden tomatoes are just turning ripe to the touch by September. But every year you can count on mornings at the farmers' markets to present bushels of crackling crisp apples, as well as an array of squash and peppers of orange, yellow, and red. All over the state, road-side stands spill over with pumpkins and dried cornstalks. Autumn is the time for Utah game, from duck to elk. It's also the beginning of soup season and time to plan a dinner party or two.

Magnificent Marinara

In or out of season, a homemade tomato sauce is a cook's best friend. In season, you can take advantage of ripe red tomatoes, bursting with flavor; out of season, a mix of fresh tomatoes and Italian plum tomatoes. This sauce may be cooked in advance and refrigerated or frozen. Spread magnificent marinara on focaccia or pizza dough to create a delicious homemade pie. Make a pink, or more substantial, sauce to top your favorite pasta by adding cream and cooked ground beef to the tomato sauce and cooking it all together at a simmer. Try our sauce with your favorite lasagna recipe or simply add shrimp for Magnificent Shrimp Marinara.

1 medium onion, chopped
2 cloves of garlic, crushed
1 cup chopped parsley or flat-leaf Italian parsley
5 mushrooms, finely chopped
$1/3$ cup olive oil
1 (28-ounce) can chopped tomatoes, or 8 large tomatoes
2 (6-ounce) cans tomato paste
$1^1/2$ cups red wine or beef broth
1 cup (or more) water
$1/2$ teaspoon sugar
$1^1/2$ teaspoons each dried oregano and basil leaves
$1/2$ teaspoon each salt and pepper

Sauté the onion, garlic, parsley and mushrooms in the olive oil in a large saucepan over medium-high heat for 3 to 5 minutes or until the mushrooms are tender.

Add the undrained tomatoes and tomato paste. Bring to a boil and stir in 1 cup of the wine. Reduce the heat to low and add the water, sugar, oregano, basil, salt and pepper.

Simmer over low heat for 20 minutes, stirring occasionally. Stir in the remaining $1/2$ cup wine and simmer for 10 minutes longer or until of the desired consistency.

Add $1/4$ to $1/2$ cup kalamata olives for a richer flavor.

Autumn
Essentials

Autumn Essentials

Homemade Chicken Stock

Stock is the essential ingredient in many classic soups, sauces, and several recipes throughout this book. Although canned broth may be substituted successfully, there is nothing as good or nutritious as the full-bodied flavor of homemade stock. Stock is simple to make and it freezes well. Use heavy-duty plastic containers and freeze it in quantities calculated for use in soups and sauces. Stock can be refrigerated for two to three days.

2 pounds chicken wings, backs, necks and bones
8 cups cold water
2 teaspoons salt
1 yellow onion, cut into chunks
3 ribs celery, cut into chunks
2 carrots, cut into chunks
1 bay leaf
8 parsley sprigs
6 peppercorns

Combine the chicken with the cold water and salt in a large saucepan. Bring to a boil and skim off the froth until no more forms. Add the onion, celery, carrots, bay leaf, parsley and peppercorns.

Simmer, loosely covered, for 2 to 3 hours or until of the desired consistency. Strain into a bowl and chill in the refrigerator. Skim the surface.

For Chicken Soup, add chopped cooked chicken and season with salt and pepper to taste. Top with chopped fresh parsley.

For Cream of Chicken Soup, also add 2 cups heated heavy cream.

For Chicken Noodle Soup, also add 1 1/2 cups cooked egg noodles.

For Chicken and Rice Soup, also add 6 tablespoons uncooked rice to the simmering stock and cook for 20 minutes or until tender, or add 1 cup cooked rice.

Roasted Chicken with Rosemary

The beauty of a roasted chicken is in its versatility. It's equally at home as part of an elegant Thanksgiving buffet or in a picnic basket at your home team's tailgate party.

1 (3-pound) chicken
salt and freshly ground pepper to taste
2 or 3 cloves of garlic, cut into halves
2 to 4 rosemary sprigs
1 teaspoon chopped fresh rosemary, or 1 to 2 teaspoons dried

Remove the giblets and neck from the chicken cavity. Rinse the chicken and pat dry. Season inside and out with a generous mixture of salt and pepper. Add the garlic and rosemary sprigs to the cavity. Pat the chopped rosemary over the outside.

Place the chicken breast side down on a rack in a roasting pan. Roast at 400 to 425 degrees for 30 minutes, basting with the pan juices. Turn the chicken breast side up and roast for 30 minutes longer or until the chicken is cooked through and the outside is brown and crisp.

For Roasted Vegetables, cut potatoes, carrots and onions into quarters, halves, or 2- to 3-inch pieces. Add to the roasting pan and sprinkle with salt and freshly ground pepper. Add a few cloves of garlic and rosemary sprigs. Roast with the chicken, tossing to coat with the pan drippings.

Essentials

Easy Pizza Dough

Based upon your own interpretation, pizza dough makes the beginning of a terrific appetizer to share with friends or a delicious dinner that is sure to please your family. It's also great for picnics, snacks, or as a table bread. This thin, flat, crusty bread is best served warm from the oven.

4 to $4^1/_2$ cups flour
2 envelopes fast-rising dry yeast
1 teaspoon sugar
2 teaspoons salt
2 teaspoons olive oil
$1^3/_4$ cups water

Mix 3 cups of the flour, yeast, sugar and salt in a large bowl. Heat the olive oil and water to 125 to 130 degrees in a small saucepan. Stir into the flour mixture with a wooden spoon; beat until smooth. Add enough of the remaining flour gradually to form a soft but firm dough.

Knead on a lightly floured surface for 8 to 10 minutes or until smooth and elastic. Let rest, covered with plastic wrap, for 10 minutes. The dough may be punched down, placed in a sealable plastic bag and stored in the refrigerator for 12 hours or frozen at this point; return to room temperature before proceeding.

Divide the dough into 8 portions for 6-inch crusts or 2 portions for large crusts. Roll the dough on a lightly oiled or cornmeal-dusted inverted baking sheet or stretch with the hands to the desired size. Bake on the lowest oven rack at 500 degrees for 10 to 14 minutes or until crisp and brown on the bottom.

For Mexican Pizza, sprinkle the dough with Monterey Jack cheese before baking and salsa after baking. Top with sour cream.

For Garden Pesto Pizza, spread the dough lightly with pesto. Top with thin slices of zucchini, yellow squash, blanched chopped broccoli, shredded mozzarella cheese and chopped tomatoes.

For Barbecue Pizza, spread barbecue sauce over the dough. Add chopped cooked chicken, scallions and shredded Gouda cheese.

For Focaccia *made from Easy Pizza Dough, increase the olive oil to 1½ tablespoons and add 2 teaspoons chopped fresh rosemary to the dough. Press indentations into the dough with the fingers or knuckles and brush with extra-virgin olive oil. Crush 2 cloves of garlic over the dough; sprinkle with kosher salt and 2 to 4 teaspoons of chopped fresh rosemary.*

Bistro Dinner

Goat Cheese with Bell Pepper Dressing
Pernod Potato and Leek Soup
Arugula and Pomegranate Salad
Pack Creek Ranch Game Hens
Vegetable Paella
Ras-Pearie Pie
Sparkling Cider
Sauvignon Blanc
Beaujolais Nouveau

Harvest Moon Supper

Pear and Bleu Cheese Salad
Curried Chicken and Pasta Soup
Brown Soda Bread
Goblin Valley Raisin Cookies
Marmalade Hill Cider
Wasatch Slick Rock Lager

Fresh pâté is a "little labor intensive," but it starts dinner with a nice impression! If you can get your butcher to bone the duck, all you'll need is a food grinder or food processor to enjoy creating a timeless recipe.

Country Duck Pâté

Ingredients
1 cup brandy
3 shallots, sliced
1 teaspoon salt
1 teaspoon pepper
2 ducks, boned
1 pound bacon
1½ pounds pork tenderloin
2 cloves of garlic, chopped
4 eggs
½ teaspoon ginger
½ teaspoon nutmeg
1 teaspoon thyme
1 teaspoon sage
1 carrot, minced
½ cup pistachios

Combine the brandy, shallots, salt and pepper in a shallow dish. Slice 3 duck breasts. Combine with the brandy mixture. Marinate in the refrigerator for 4 hours.

Grind the remaining duck, bacon, pork and garlic very fine. Combine with the eggs, ginger, nutmeg, thyme and sage in a bowl and mix well. Add the carrot and pistachios and mix well.

Layer half the ground mixture, the marinated duck and the remaining ground mixture in a greased terrine pan; cover with foil. Place in a larger pan of water. Bake at 325 degrees for 2½ hours or to an internal temperature of 150 degrees. Invert onto a plate and slice to serve.

Serves Twelve to Fifteen

A melange of red, yellow, and green bell peppers is always an appetizing sight. They team up here with the fresh and slightly tangy taste of goat cheese, which has a creamy texture, yet is relatively low in fat.

Goat Cheese with Bell Pepper Dressing

Sauté the bell peppers in 1 tablespoon heated olive oil in a heavy skillet for 5 minutes or until tender. Add the remaining 3 tablespoons olive oil, garlic, rosemary, coriander seeds, fennel seeds, thyme, bay leaf and pepper and mix well. Simmer for 5 minutes. Remove from the heat and season with salt. Cool to room temperature; discard the bay leaf.

Spread the goat cheese on a platter. Spoon the pepper dressing over the top. Let stand for 1 hour. Sprinkle with the pine nuts. Serve at room temperature with baguette slices.

Serves Four

Ingredients

1 green bell pepper, chopped
1 red bell pepper, chopped
1 yellow bell pepper, chopped
1/4 cup olive oil
4 large cloves of garlic, chopped
3/4 teaspoon dried rosemary
1/2 teaspoon crushed coriander seeds
1/4 teaspoon crushed fennel seeds
1/4 teaspoon dried thyme
1 bay leaf
1/4 teaspoon freshly ground pepper
salt to taste
8 ounces chilled Montrachet or other goat cheese
2 tablespoons toasted pine nuts
toasted baguette slices

Butternut squash makes a wonderful base for soup. Teamed with ripe pears, tart apples, sage, and nutmeg, it absolutely shines with autumn flavors. In addition to seafood, bisque can also define a soup of vegetable purée, smoothed out with a splash of sherry.

Butternut Harvest Bisque

Ingredients
1 (3-pound) butternut
   squash
1 large onion, chopped
2½ tablespoons butter
2 large tart apples, peeled,
   chopped
1 large ripe Bartlett pear,
   peeled, chopped
3½ cups chicken broth
2 teaspoons fresh thyme
1 teaspoon fresh sage
⅛ teaspoon nutmeg
1 bay leaf
½ teaspoon salt
½ teaspoon pepper
½ to 1 cup half-and-half
3 tablespoons sherry
   (optional)

Garnish
2 tablespoons finely
   chopped walnuts

Cut the squash into halves lengthwise and discard the seeds. Peel with a vegetable peeler and cut into 1½-inch chunks.

Sauté the onion in the butter in a 4-quart saucepan over medium-high heat for 4 minutes or until tender. Add the squash, apples, pear and chicken broth.

Add the thyme, sage, nutmeg, bay leaf, salt and pepper to the saucepan. Bring to a boil over medium-high heat and reduce the heat. Simmer for 20 minutes or until the squash is very tender. Cool to room temperature; discard the bay leaf.

Purée the mixture in 3 or 4 batches in a food processor. Combine in a clean saucepan. Stir in the half-and-half and sherry. Adjust the seasonings. Heat just to the simmering stage; do not boil.

Ladle into soup bowls. Garnish with the walnuts.

Serves Seven or Eight

Curried Chicken and Pasta Soup

Heat the oil in a large enamel saucepan. Add the chicken, onion, garlic, bell pepper, curry powder, ginger and red pepper. Sauté until the chicken is opaque and the onion is tender.

Stir in the chicken broth and undrained tomatoes and bring just to the boiling point. Add the apples, pasta and currants and reduce the heat. Simmer until the pasta is al dente and the chicken is cooked through.

Ladle into soup bowls. Garnish with yogurt and cilantro sprigs.

Serves Six

Ingredients
1 tablespoon vegetable oil
1 pound chicken tenders, sliced
1 large yellow onion, chopped
5 cloves of garlic, crushed
1 medium red bell pepper, chopped
1 tablespoon curry powder
1 tablespoon grated fresh ginger
$1/2$ teaspoon red pepper
4 cups chicken broth
2 cups chopped peeled tomatoes, or 1 (16-ounce) can tomatoes
2 large Granny Smith apples, peeled, chopped
$1/2$ cup uncooked orzo
$1/4$ cup currants or raisins

Garnish
plain yogurt
cilantro sprigs

umn

The faint anise-like character of Pernod and fennel create a beguiling flavor combination in this elegant leek and potato soup for a chilly night.

Potato and Leek Soup with Pernod

Ingredients

2 fennel bulbs (about
    1 pound) with 2 inches
    stalk
2 medium leeks
2 medium baking potatoes
    (about 1 pound)
3 tablespoons unsalted
    butter
1 tablespoon vegetable oil
2 quarts chicken stock
1/4 cup Pernod (optional)
1 teaspoon salt
1/2 teaspoon finely ground
    white pepper

Remove the core from the fennel bulbs and slice the bulbs, reserving some of the sprigs for garnish. Clean and coarsely chop the white parts only of the leeks. Peel and coarsely chop the potatoes.

Heat the butter and oil in a medium saucepan over low heat. Add the leeks and sauté until tender. Add the fennel and potatoes. Sauté for 10 minutes longer or until tender. Stir in the chicken stock and bring to a simmer. Simmer, loosely covered, for 30 minutes.

Purée the mixture in a food processor or blender. Combine with the Pernod, salt and white pepper in the saucepan. Simmer until heated through. Adjust the seasonings.

Ladle into soup bowls. Top with the reserved fennel sprigs.

Serves Six to Eight

Autumn

Chefs tell us that when cooking with wine or spirits we should never use anything that we wouldn't drink. If the alcoholic ingredients are inferior, cooking will just bring out the worst in their flavors. You don't have to cook with the same expensive wine that you are serving for dinner, however. Instead, ask your wine merchant for a recommendation of something less expensive with similar qualities. Cooking reduces, rather than eliminates, alcoholic content, so if you don't want any trace of alcohol in your dish, don't use it.

Arugula and Pomegranate Salad

For the vinaigrette, combine the vinegar and mustard in a small bowl or jar with a lid and mix well. Add the sugar and salt gradually, mixing or shaking after each addition until dissolved. Whisk in the olive oil gradually or add to the jar and shake to mix. Store in the refrigerator for up to 1 week.

For the salad, spread the pecans on a baking sheet. Bake at 350 degrees for 6 minutes. Cool to room temperature.

Combine the arugula, pomegranate seeds, avocado and pecans in a bowl. Add the vinaigrette and toss to mix well. Serve immediately.

Serves Six

Mustard Vinaigrette
1/3 cup balsamic vinegar
1 teaspoon Dijon mustard
1/4 teaspoon sugar
1/2 teaspoon salt
2/3 cup olive oil

Salad
1/2 cup pecans
2 (4-ounce) packages
    arugula, or 6 cups
    arugula, trimmed
3/4 cup pomegranate seeds
1 avocado, chopped

Edible flower mixes—to be used for salads and for garnishes—are making their way into supermarket produce sections in Utah and all over the country. If you pick your own edibles, make sure that they are indeed edible by checking with a botanist (try the Red Butte Gardens in Salt Lake City), and make sure that they are carefully washed and have not been sprayed with toxic substances. Among the most familiar varieties of edibles are nasturtiums, which have a slightly peppery bite; they are good over a salad of mesclun and watercress. You can also try chive blossoms; violas, pansies, and violets; plum, peach, and squash blossoms; scented geraniums; and marigolds.

*Use Maytag bleu cheese for this salad if it is available.
It is considered the best American bleu cheese.*

Pear and Bleu Cheese Salad

Raspberry Vinaigrette
1/4 cup raspberry vinegar
1 tablespoon Dijon mustard
1 teaspoon sugar
1/2 cup plus 2 tablespoons
    light extra-virgin
    olive oil
salt and pepper to taste

Salad
1/4 cup chopped walnuts
6 to 8 cups mixed greens,
    such as escarole, butter
    lettuce or red leaf lettuce
1 cup chopped or sliced
    Bosc or Anjou pear
4 ounces bleu cheese,
    crumbled

For the vinaigrette, combine the raspberry vinegar, mustard and sugar in a small bowl. Whisk in the olive oil very gradually. Season with salt and pepper to taste.

For the salad, spread the walnuts on a baking sheet. Toast at 300 degrees for 5 minutes. Cool to room temperature.

Combine the greens, pear and bleu cheese in a salad bowl. Add the desired amount of vinaigrette and toss gently to mix. Top with the walnuts.

Serves Six to Eight

Sweet Utah pears and salty fragrant bleu cheese were made for each other. Pears are usually sold green because they are one of the few fruits that do not ripen on the tree. But you don't want to eat them until they are ripe—just at the point when they achieve that silky smooth texture and ambrosial flavor. To speed the ripening process, place pears in a paper bag, close it, and let stand at room temperature for a couple of days. Pears are usually available through the fall in Utah. Look for Bartlett, Anjou, Bosc, and Comice.

Flank Steak Tournedos Hollandaise

Pound the flank steak to ¹/₂-inch thickness. Add meat tenderizer using the package directions. Sprinkle the steak with garlic salt and pepper. Score diagonally into diamond shapes.

Fry the bacon in a skillet until almost cooked but still flexible; drain. Arrange the bacon lengthwise on the steak; sprinkle with the parsley.

Roll the steak from the narrow end to enclose the bacon; secure with skewers at 1-inch intervals. Cut into 1-inch slices with a serrated knife. Grill the steaks over medium coals for 15 minutes for rare, turning once.

Add the tarragon to the dry hollandaise sauce mix. Prepare the mix using the package directions. Serve with the steaks.

Serves Four to Eight

Ingredients

1 (1- to 1¹/₂-pound) flank
   steak
nonseasoned meat
   tenderizer
1 teaspoon garlic salt
¹/₂ teaspoon freshly ground
   pepper
8 ounces sliced bacon
2 tablespoons chopped
   parsley
¹/₄ teaspoon dried tarragon,
   crushed
1 envelope hollandaise
   sauce mix

Veal Scaloppine

Ingredients
¹/₄ cup flour
1 teaspoon salt
¹/₂ teaspoon pepper
1 pound veal, cubed
2 tablespoons chopped
    onion
2 tablespoons olive oil or
    butter
1 cup chicken stock
¹/₂ cup mushrooms
1¹/₂ teaspoons lemon juice

Garnish
¹/₄ cup chopped parsley

Mix the flour, salt and pepper in a sealable plastic or nonrecycled paper bag. Add the veal cubes and shake to coat well.

Sauté the onion in the heated olive oil in a skillet until light brown. Add the veal and cook until brown on all sides.

Add the chicken stock and mushrooms. Simmer, covered, for 30 minutes or longer. Stir in the lemon juice just before serving. Serve over rice with a green salad and Italian bread. Garnish with the parsley.

Serves Two to Four

Spicy Grilled Pork

Ingredients
1 (1-inch) piece fresh
    ginger, peeled, minced
1 jalapeño pepper, seeded,
    minced
¹/₃ cup honey
3 tablespoons soy sauce
3 tablespoons sesame oil
¹/₄ teaspoon red pepper
    flakes, crushed
2 (12-ounce) pork
    tenderloins

Combine the ginger, jalapeño pepper, honey, soy sauce, sesame oil and pepper flakes in a bowl. Reserve and chill ¹/₃ of the mixture for basting. Combine the remaining mixture with the pork in a sealable plastic bag. Marinate the pork in the refrigerator for 2 to 12 hours.

To grill, drain the pork and place on a rack sprayed with nonstick cooking spray and place over medium-hot coals. Grill for 10 minutes, turning once and basting with the reserved basting sauce.

To broil, drain the pork and place on a rack in a broiler pan. Broil 6 inches from the heat source for 8 to 10 minutes or until cooked through, turning once and basting with the reserved basting sauce.

Serve with rice and sautéed snow peas.

Serves Four to Six

Pasta with Sausage and Tomato Cream Sauce

Remove the sausage casings. Brown the sausage in the butter in a large skillet. Remove the sausage with a slotted spoon and drain the skillet.

Add the cream, tomato paste, wine, parsley, nutmeg and half the Parmesan cheese to the skillet and stir to deglaze. Add the sausage. Simmer for 3 to 4 minutes.

Cook the pasta al dente using the package directions; drain. Combine the pasta with 2 tablespoons of the sauce and the remaining Parmesan cheese in a serving bowl; toss to coat well. Pour the remaining sauce over the top. Garnish with the parsley.

Serves Six

Ingredients
12 ounces sweet Italian
    sausage
12 ounces hot Italian
    sausage
$1/4$ cup butter
2 cups heavy cream
1 (6-ounce) can tomato
    paste
1 cup dry white wine
2 tablespoons minced fresh
    parsley
$1/2$ teaspoon nutmeg
1 cup grated Parmesan
    cheese
12 ounces uncooked pasta

Garnish
1 tablespoon chopped fresh
    parsley

Acorn Squash over Wild Rice and Sausage

Wild Rice and Sausage
8 ounces Italian pork
    sausage, crumbled
1 small onion, coarsely
    chopped
2 cups cooked wild rice
3 or 4 fresh sage leaves,
    minced, or 1/2 teaspoon
    dried
1 teaspoon minced fresh
    marjoram, or
    1/2 teaspoon dried
salt and pepper to taste

Squash
8 ounces small Brussels
    sprouts
2 medium acorn squash
1 tablespoon melted butter
juice of 1 lemon wedge
grated nutmeg to taste

For the rice and sausage, brown the sausage in a skillet, stirring until crumbly. Add the onion. Cook for 10 minutes; drain. Add the rice, sage, marjoram, salt and pepper and mix well. Spoon into a shallow 3-quart baking dish.

For the squash, steam the Brussels sprouts for 5 to 8 minutes or until tender. Cut the squash into quarters, discarding the seeds. Steam for 8 to 10 minutes or until tender.

Arrange the squash on the rice and sausage mixture. Spoon the Brussels sprouts into the squash cavities. Drizzle with the melted butter and lemon juice. Sprinkle with nutmeg. Chill, covered with foil, at this point if desired. Bake, covered, at 350 degrees for 15 to 20 minutes or until heated through.

Serves Six

Ground buffalo meat makes an especially smooth tender meatloaf when combined with pork in Chef Tim Buckingham's recipe.

Buck's Grill House Buffalo Meatloaf

Sauté the onion, carrot, celery and bell pepper in the oil until the onion is translucent. Add the Spice Rub and cook for 5 minutes longer. Spoon into a large bowl and cool to room temperature.

Add the catsup, cream, eggs, Worcestershire sauce, oats, bread crumbs, buffalo and pork; mix well by hand. Pack into a lightly oiled loaf pan and strike the bottom of the pan on the counter to release trapped air. Bake at 375 degrees for 1¼ hours or to 160 degrees on a meat thermometer.

Cool in the pan for 15 minutes. Remove to a serving plate. Slice and serve warm with Black Onion Gravy.

Serves Eight

For Spice Rub, combine ¼ cup each of sugar, brown sugar, chili powder, cumin, Mexican oregano, kosher salt and pepper. Add ¾ cup paprika and mix well. Store in an airtight container.

For Black Onion Gravy, sauté 4 cups chopped onions in ¼ cup oil over high heat until the onions are brown. Add ¼ cup Spice Rub and cook for 10 minutes longer. Add ½ cup soy sauce and bring to a simmer. Whisk in ½ cup flour and simmer over medium heat for 10 minutes. Whisk in 1 quart of homemade veal stock or canned beef broth. Simmer for 15 minutes or until thickened, stirring until smooth.

Ingredients

Ingredients
1 cup chopped onion
½ cup chopped carrot
½ cup chopped celery
½ cup chopped red bell pepper
¼ cup vegetable oil
¼ cup Spice Rub
⅓ cup catsup
⅓ cup cream
2 large eggs
2 tablespoons Worcestershire sauce
¾ cup rolled oats
¾ cup dry bread crumbs
2 pounds ground buffalo
8 ounces ground pork

Chef Tim Buckingham is a Moab native who left Utah to pursue culinary studies and to work in the southern California wine country. Then he came back to his hometown near Arches National Park and was one of the first chefs to open a knock-out, uptown restaurant in a small town known far and wide for its outdoor attractions but not exactly renowned for sophisticated dining. Buck's Grill House is his second Moab restaurant and features creative American Western food.

Deep Creek Ranch Fajitas

Tequila Marinade
2 ounces (¹/₄ cup) gold
    tequila
2 tablespoons olive oil
1 tablespoon fresh lime
    juice
2 (or more) cloves of garlic,
    minced
¹/₂ cup loosely packed
    chopped fresh cilantro
1 to 2 serrano or jalapeño
    peppers, minced
1 teaspoon cumin
¹/₂ teaspoon oregano

Fajitas
1¹/₂ pounds elk steak
2 green bell peppers, sliced
1 red bell pepper, sliced
1 yellow bell pepper, sliced
2 onions, sliced

For the marinade, combine the tequila, olive oil, lime juice, garlic, cilantro, serrano peppers, cumin and oregano in a shallow dish. Reserve and chill half the mixture.

Cut the elk across the grain into thin slices. Add to the remaining marinade. Marinate, covered, in the refrigerator for 6 to 8 hours; drain.

Grill the elk until cooked through. Keep warm.

Combine the reserved marinade with the bell peppers and onions in a skillet. Cook until the peppers and onions are tender and the liquid is reduced.

Serve the elk and vegetables with warm tortillas, jalapeños and green tomatillo sauce.

To cook on the stove top, cook the drained elk in the reserved marinade and remove with a slotted spoon. Cook the vegetables as above, return the elk to the skillet and cook just until heated through.

This dish can also be prepared with beef or chicken.

Serves Eight

Aspen at sunrise
Sunset Point, Bryce Canyon National Park

Canyonlands Chicken Potpie

Ingredients

4 boneless skinless chicken
   breast halves
$1/2$ cup chicken broth
$1/2$ pound thin-skinned
   potatoes, chopped
3 tablespoons cornstarch
$1/2$ cup chicken broth
1 (15-ounce) can stewed
   chopped tomatoes
1 (15-ounce) can black
   beans, rinsed, drained
1 (8-ounce) can corn
   kernels, drained
1 (4-ounce) can chopped
   green chiles
$1/2$ cup chopped fresh
   cilantro
1 unbaked pie pastry, at
   room temperature

Cut the chicken into $3/4$-inch cubes. Combine with $1/2$ cup chicken broth and potatoes in a 12-inch skillet. Cook over medium-high heat for 5 minutes or until the chicken is opaque and just until the potatoes are tender.

Blend the cornstarch with $1/2$ cup chicken broth in a small bowl. Stir into the chicken mixture. Bring to a boil, stirring constantly; remove from the heat. Add the undrained tomatoes, beans, corn, green chiles and cilantro. Pour into a 10-inch pie plate or $1^{1/2}$-quart baking dish.

Roll the pastry into a 12-inch circle for a pie plate, or 1 inch larger than a baking dish. Place over the chicken mixture; fold under and flute the edge and cut vents. Top with shapes cut from the remaining pastry.

Bake at 350 degrees for 1 hour or until the filling is bubbly and the crust is golden brown. Cover with foil if necessary to prevent overbrowning. Cool for 10 minutes before serving.

Serves Four

Autumn

Sundance Chicken Hash

Heat a large nonstick sauté pan over high heat. Add the clarified butter and potatoes. Cook until well browned, tossing occasionally.

Reduce the heat to medium and add the onion. Sauté for 3 to 4 minutes or until tender. Add the bell pepper and chicken and cook until heated through. Add the scallions, parsley, salt and pepper.

Mound onto 6 serving plates. Top each serving with an egg.

Serves Six

Ingredients
2 tablespoons clarified
    butter or vegetable oil
3 cups (1/2-inch) peeled
    potato cubes
3/4 cup (1/2-inch) red onion
    pieces
3/4 cup (1/2-inch) peeled
    roasted red bell pepper
    pieces
1 cup shredded roasted
    chicken
1/4 cup minced scallions
1 tablespoon chopped
    parsley
salt and pepper to taste
6 large eggs, cooked as
    you like

Sundance Resort is a gorgeous oasis in a great forest, best known for access to Alpine and Nordic skiing, snowshoeing, and fly-fishing. All of these activities, plus independent film and theater workshops and summer theater performances, take place within view of magnificent Mt. Timpanagos in Provo Canyon. Sundance is also one of Utah's nationally acclaimed dining destinations. Foods served in the Foundry Grill represent the best of fresh American home-style cooking, often created over a wood-fire grill with fresh ingredients from Sundance's own gardens and local purveyors. This is Chef Trey Foshee's version of comfort food.

Not your everyday spaghetti sauce, this one is made with ground turkey and spiced up with a few shakes of chili powder and anchovy paste—a supreme secret ingredient.

Ron's Supreme Spaghetti Sauce

Brown the ground turkey with the onion and garlic in the olive oil in an 8-quart saucepan, stirring until the turkey is crumbly.

Add the mushrooms, tomatoes, tomato sauce, tomato paste, anchovy paste, basil, oregano, parsley, sugar, garlic powder, chili powder, vegetable salt and pepper. Simmer for 2 to 3 hours.

Serve over spaghetti or linguine with freshly grated Parmesan cheese, green salad and French bread.

Serves Twelve

Ingredients

1 pound ground turkey

1 large red or yellow onion, chopped

2 cloves of garlic, pressed

1/4 cup olive oil

8 ounces sliced fresh mushrooms, or 1 large can stems and pieces

8 cups peeled, seeded, chopped tomatoes, or 1 (28-ounce) can chopped tomatoes

1 (15-ounce) can tomato sauce

2 (6-ounce) cans tomato paste

1 inch anchovy paste from a tube

2 to 3 tablespoons chopped fresh basil, or 1 tablespoon dried

1 tablespoon chopped fresh oregano, or 1/2 tablespoon dried

1/3 cup chopped fresh parsley

1 1/2 tablespoons sugar

1/4 teaspoon garlic powder

6 to 8 shakes chili powder or cayenne

1/4 teaspoon vegetable or sea salt

freshly ground pepper to taste

Utahns love tomatoes, and when they need to peel fresh tomatoes for cooked dishes, they have learned that there is only one way to go. Put a big pot of water on to boil. Cut a shallow X in the bottom of each tomato and place two at a time in the water with a slotted spoon. Leave just 5 seconds for ripe tomatoes and 10 seconds for less ripe. Remove, drain and cool slightly, and slip the skins off. To seed fresh tomatoes, cut into halves horizontally and place cut side down in a strainer over a bowl. Squeeze out the seeds gently. The strainer will catch the seeds and you can keep the juice to add to sauces, soups, and salad dressings.

*Enjoy this no-fail version of duck a l'orange from
Pack Creek Ranch in Moab.*

Pack Creek Ranch Game Hens

For the game hens, remove the giblets and necks and rinse the hens inside and out under cold running water; pat dry. Place the onion and celery in the cavities. Tuck the wing tips behind the backs and truss the legs with string.

Place in a baking pan. Brush with melted butter and sprinkle with paprika. Roast at 325 degrees for 1 hour or until cooked through.

For the sauce, combine the chicken broth, orange marmalade and orange juice concentrate in a saucepan. Blend the cornstarch with the cold water in a small bowl. Stir into the orange mixture. Cook until thickened and smooth, stirring constantly. Serve with the game hens.

Serves Six

Game Hens
6 game hens
1 medium onion, cut into 6
   wedges
6 ribs celery heart with
   leaves
melted butter
paprika to taste

Orange Sauce
1 (14-ounce) can chicken
   broth
1 cup orange marmalade
1/4 cup frozen orange juice
   concentrate, thawed
2 tablespoons cornstarch
1/2 cup cold water

Jane Sleight of Pack Creek Ranch suggests you serve these sweet orange-glazed game hens with wild rice seasoned with a blend of mushrooms, finely diced onion, pepper, and sage sautéed in butter.

Almond-Crusted Salmon with Red Butter Sauce

Salmon
1 pound blanched slivered
    almonds
8 (7-ounce) salmon fillets
salt and pepper to taste
¼ cup vegetable oil

Red Butter Sauce
1 cup chopped shallots
2 cups red wine
2 bay leaves
¼ cup heavy cream
2 pounds butter, at room
    temperature, chopped
salt and pepper to taste

For the salmon, grind the almonds fine in a food processor. Sprinkle the salmon with salt and pepper. Coat the meaty side with the almonds. Sear almond side down in the oil in a nonstick skillet over medium heat until the almonds are golden brown. Turn the fillets and cook for several minutes or until cooked through. Remove to a baking sheet.

For the sauce, combine the shallots, red wine and bay leaves in a saucepan. Cook until almost completely reduced. Add the cream and cook until slightly reduced. Reduce the heat to medium. Whisk in the butter. Season with salt and pepper. Discard the bay leaves and keep the sauce warm.

Reheat the salmon in a 400-degree oven. Serve with the sauce. Add potatoes and wilted spinach for a complete meal.

Serves Eight

Shallots are especially good in sauces such as this one. They look like tiny onions with a golden husk, but are milder and sweeter than regular onions. Avoid shallots and garlic that are sprouting, as they are past their prime and will have a mushy texture and bitter flavor.

Autumn

Linguine with Salmon and Mushrooms

Cook the linguine using the package directions; keep warm.

Cut the salmon into 3/4-inch pieces. Season with salt and pepper. Sauté in the heated olive oil in a heavy large skillet for 3 minutes or just until cooked through. Remove with a slotted spoon.

Add the garlic to the skillet and sauté for 30 seconds. Add the mushrooms and sauté for 2 minutes. Add the green onions, tomato, wine and capers. Cook for 5 minutes or until the mushrooms are tender.

Combine the salmon, sautéed vegetables and drained linguine in a large bowl. Add the lemon juice and dill and toss to mix well. Season with salt and pepper to taste.

Garnish with lemon slices or dill. Serve with a salad and crusty bread.

Serves Four

Ingredients

8 ounces uncooked linguine

1 (12-ounce) skinless salmon fillet

salt and pepper to taste

1/4 cup olive oil

3 large cloves of garlic, minced

8 ounces mushrooms, sliced

5 green onions, chopped

1 large tomato, seeded, chopped

1/3 cup dry white wine

3 tablespoons drained capers

1 tablespoon fresh lemon juice

1/4 cup chopped fresh dill

Garnish

lemon slices or fresh dill

As an international airline hub of the intermountain West, Salt Lake City gets daily fresh shipments of seafood from around the world for recipes such as this one.

Serve Vegetable Paella as an accompaniment to meats or fish, with a salad as a light supper, or with chicken or shrimp added for a hearty main dish. To serve it at room temperature, drizzle it with lemon juice and olive oil.

Vegetable Paella

Heat the olive oil in a deep 12-inch cast-iron skillet over medium heat. Add the green chile, onion and bell peppers and reduce the heat to medium-low. Cook for 20 minutes or until the vegetables are tender and the onion is light brown.

Add the garlic, zucchini, tomatoes, paprika, thyme, salt and pepper. Simmer, covered, for 15 minutes.

Stir in the rice and chicken stock and bring to a boil. Reduce the heat to medium-low. Simmer, covered, for 20 to 25 minutes or until the rice is tender. Correct the seasoning. Garnish with parsley.

Serves Four to Six

Ingredients
1/4 cup olive oil
1 small fresh green chile
    pepper, minced
1 large white onion, cut
    into quarters, thinly
    sliced
1 large red bell pepper,
    chopped
1 large yellow bell pepper,
    chopped
1 large green bell pepper,
    chopped
2 large cloves of garlic,
    minced
1 medium zucchini,
    chopped
4 large tomatoes, peeled,
    seeded, chopped
1 1/2 teaspoons Hungarian
    paprika
1 tablespoon fresh thyme
    leaves
salt and pepper to taste
1 1/4 cups uncooked arborio
    rice
2 cups chicken stock

Garnish
finely minced parsley

The secret of perfect paella is the rice. Use short grain rice and cook it uncovered to prevent steaming. Don't wait until the rice looks done. It should finish cooking away from the heat to retain its shape and texture.

Simply delicious and brightly colored, this makes an excellent meatless entrée. It is also a wonderful way to use the garden zucchini that may be coming out of your ears by early autumn.

Park City Penne with Zucchini Cream

Cut the zucchini into halves lengthwise and then diagonally into $1/8$-inch slices. Add the onion and garlic to the heated butter in a saucepan and sauté until the onion is tender. Add the zucchini and sauté for 1 minute. Stir in the whipping cream and milk. Simmer for 1 minute.

Cook the pasta al dente using the package directions; drain. Add to the zucchini mixture with the sun-dried tomatoes, basil and Parmesan cheese; mix gently. Cook just until heated through.

Serve immediately. Garnish with Parmesan cheese.

Serves Four

Ingredients
4 medium zucchini
1 medium onion, thinly
   sliced
1 clove of garlic, minced
$1/4$ cup butter
$1^1/4$ cups whipping cream
$1/2$ cup milk
$2/3$ pound uncooked penne
$1/2$ cup sliced drained sun-
   dried tomatoes
$3/4$ cup shredded fresh basil
$3/4$ cup grated Parmesan
   cheese

Garnish
grated Parmesan cheese

Slick Rock Garden Pasta

Ingredients
1 portobello mushroom,
    sliced ½ inch thick
12 ounces uncooked
    linguine
3 tablespoons olive oil
3 tablespoons minced garlic
4 shallots, thinly sliced
2 tablespoons dry white
    wine
3 cups chopped Roma
    tomatoes
2 ounces fresh basil strips
1 teaspoon salt
½ teaspoon pepper

Garnish
½ cup grated Parmesan
    cheese

Grill or boil the mushroom in water until tender. Cut into bite-size pieces. Cook the linguine using the package directions; drain and keep warm.

Heat the olive oil in a 12-inch skillet. Add the garlic and shallots and sauté until the shallots are translucent but not brown.

Add the wine, stirring to deglaze the skillet. Cook until the wine is slightly reduced. Add the tomatoes. Cook until the mixture is reduced to the desired consistency. Stir in the mushroom, basil, salt and pepper.

Place the linguine on serving plates. Spoon the sauce over the top. Garnish with the Parmesan cheese.

Serves Four

Slick Rock Trail, Porcupine Rim, Kokopelli's, and miles of other fat-tire-friendly redrock trails around the town of Moab attract serious cyclists from all over the world. They like to refuel at the colorful Slick Rock Cafe, where this light but sophisticated garden pasta is a favorite.

Vegetarian Tostadas with Avocado and Cheese

Brush the tortillas on both sides with ¹/₂ tablespoon olive oil and place on a baking sheet. Bake at 375 degrees for 6 to 8 minutes or until crisp.

Combine the lettuce, tomato and jalapeño pepper in a medium bowl. Combine the vinegar, water, 1 tablespoon olive oil, salt and black pepper in a small bowl and whisk until smooth. Add to the lettuce mixture and toss to mix well.

Spread 1 tablespoon of beans over each tortilla. Spread 2 tablespoons of avocado over the beans. Top with the lettuce mixture. Sprinkle with the cheese, olives and onion rings.

Serves Four

Ingredients
4 (6-inch) flour tortillas
¹/₂ tablespoon olive oil
1 cup finely shredded lettuce
¹/₄ cup chopped tomato
2 teaspoons chopped jalapeño pepper
1¹/₂ teaspoons red wine vinegar
4 teaspoons water
1 tablespoon olive oil
¹/₄ teaspoon salt
¹/₈ teaspoon freshly ground black pepper
¹/₄ cup vegetarian refried beans
¹/₂ cup mashed avocado
¹/₄ cup crumbled cheese
6 pitted olives, thinly sliced
4 thin slices sweet onion

The combination of garlic and pine nuts with roasted green beans gives this ordinary vegetable an updated flavor for autumn.

Roasted Green Beans with Garlic and Pine Nuts

Ingredients
2 tablespoons olive oil
1 pound fresh green beans,
    trimmed
1 cup thinly sliced onion
10 to 12 medium cloves of
    garlic
salt and pepper to taste
1 to 2 tablespoons balsamic
    or red wine vinegar
1 cup lightly toasted
    pine nuts

Brush a large baking sheet with the olive oil. Spread the green beans, onion and garlic on the prepared baking sheet. Sprinkle with salt and pepper. Roast at 400 degrees for 20 to 30 minutes or until as tender as desired, shaking the baking sheet occasionally.

Spoon the bean mixture into a serving bowl. Drizzle with the vinegar and sprinkle with pepper. Top with the pine nuts. Serve at any temperature.

Serves Six

Carrot Puff

Ingredients
1 pound carrots
3/4 to 1 cup milk
3 eggs, beaten
1/2 cup sugar
2 tablespoons flour
1 tablespoon baking
    powder
1/4 teaspoon cinnamon
1/2 cup melted butter

Garnish
grated carrots or twisted
    orange slices

Cut the carrots into 1-inch pieces. Cook in water to cover in a saucepan until tender; drain. Process with the milk in a food processor until smooth.

Combine with the eggs, sugar, flour, baking powder and cinnamon in a bowl and mix well. Add the butter and mix lightly.

Spoon into a 1- to 1 1/2-quart baking dish. Bake at 350 degrees for 30 minutes or until the center is set and springs back when lightly touched. Garnish with grated carrots or orange slices.

Serves Four to Six

Autumn

Red Cabbage with Wine

Cut the cabbage into quarters, discarding the cores and outer leaves. Coarsely shred the cabbage. Combine with the wine, brown sugar, apples, salt and cayenne in a saucepan.

Simmer, covered, for 30 minutes or until the cabbage is tender. Add the vinegar and butter and toss until the butter melts.

Serve as a colorful savory side dish with pork.

Serves Six

Ingredients
1 (2-pound) head red
    cabbage
1 cup red wine
1/3 cup packed brown sugar
4 medium apples, peeled,
    cut into quarters, cored
1 teaspoon salt
cayenne to taste
1/4 cup cider vinegar
1/4 cup butter

Torrey Corn Pie

Cream the margarine and sugar in a mixer bowl until light and fluffy. Beat in the eggs 1 at a time.

Add the flour, cornmeal and baking powder and mix until smooth. Stir in the green chiles, corn and cheese.

Spoon into a greased 9x13-inch baking pan. Bake at 300 degrees for 1 hour. Serve with chili.

Serves Eight to Twelve

Ingredients
1/2 cup margarine, softened
1 cup sugar
4 eggs
1 cup flour
1 cup yellow or blue
    cornmeal
4 teaspoons baking powder
1 (4-ounce) can chopped
    green chiles
1 (16-ounce) can cream-
    style corn
1 cup shredded Cheddar or
    Monterey Jack cheese

The quiet community of Torrey exemplifies the beauty of unspoiled Utah towns located near some of the most stunning scenery in the world. From Torrey, it's a short drive into Capitol Reef National Park, with its red rock formations such as the massive Temples of the Moon and Sun. It's also a short drive to scenic Byway 12—a perfect vantage point for some stunning views, including the tip of the 1.7-million-acre Grand Staircase-Escalante National Monument.

This is an excellent accompaniment to steaks, lamb chops, or roasted chicken.

Scalloped Potatoes with Leeks and Cream

Ingredients

2 pounds leeks
1/4 cup unsalted butter
salt and pepper to taste
2 cups whipping cream
3 large cloves of garlic,
   minced
4 pounds russet potatoes,
   peeled, thinly sliced
2 cups shredded white
   Cheddar or Swiss cheese
1/3 cup grated Parmesan
   cheese

Slice enough of the white and pale green portions only of the leeks to measure 4 cups. Melt the butter in a heavy saucepan over medium-high heat. Add the leeks and stir to coat well; reduce the heat. Cook, covered, for 8 minutes or until the leeks are tender, stirring occasionally. Cook, uncovered, until the liquid is absorbed. Season with salt and pepper.

Mix the whipping cream and garlic in a small bowl. Layer half the potatoes in a buttered 9x13-inch baking dish and sprinkle with salt and pepper. Layer half the leeks and half the Cheddar cheese over the potatoes. Spoon half the cream mixture over the layers. Repeat the layers and top with the Parmesan cheese.

Bake at 375 degrees for 1 1/4 hours or until the top is deep golden brown.

Serves Six

Maples at Stewart Cascades
Sundance Area, Mount Timpanagus Wilderness

This recipe combines three of the most wonderful autumn ingredients. Leeks are delicate in flavor, parsnips are slightly sweet and almost nut-like, and carrots add both color and flavor. Dijon mustard cuts the cream and gives the dish a French profile.

Parsnip and Leek Gratin with Carrots

Ingredients

2 pounds leeks
1½ pounds large carrots
1½ pounds large parsnips
2 tablespoons butter
salt to taste
2½ cups whipping cream
2 teaspoons Dijon mustard
2 tablespoons chopped
    fresh sage, or
    2 teaspoons rubbed
    dried
¾ teaspoon salt
½ teaspoon pepper
½ cup coarsely grated
    Parmesan cheese

Trim the leeks, keeping only the white and pale green portions. Cut into halves, rinse and slice crosswise into 1-inch pieces. Peel the carrots and parsnips and cut diagonally into ¼-inch slices.

Sauté the leeks in the butter in a large heavy skillet over medium-low heat for 15 minutes or just until tender and light brown. Spoon into a large bowl.

Combine the carrots and parsnips with salt to taste in boiling water in a large saucepan. Cook for 3 minutes or until tender-crisp; drain. Add to the leeks.

Whisk the whipping cream with the mustard, sage, ¾ teaspoon salt and pepper in a medium bowl. Add to the vegetables and mix gently.

Spoon the mixture into a buttered 9x13-inch baking dish. Sprinkle with the cheese. Cover with foil. Chill for up to 6 hours at this point if desired; return to room temperature before baking.

Bake, covered, on a rack in the top third of the oven at 400 degrees for 30 minutes. Bake, uncovered, for 30 minutes longer or until the top is golden brown and the cream has thickened. Let stand for 10 minutes. Serve hot.

Serves Six to Eight

Autumn

Utah's autumn leeks are the aristocrats of onions. Still-life painters and great chefs have long adored the mild green onions that look like giant scallions. So, why don't more home cooks enjoy them? Maybe because they have heard leeks are hard to clean, but there is an easy way to remove the dirt that wedges inside the tight layers of the bulb ends. Slice 1 inch off the top and ½ inch off the bottom of each leek. Cut into halves lengthwise and wash under cold water.

Sweet Potato and Apple Scallop is a scrumptious side dish that captures the very essence of autumn.

Sweet Potato and Apple Scallop

Cook the sweet potatoes in water to cover for 15 minutes or until tender-crisp. Peel and slice ¼ inch thick.

Layer half the sweet potatoes, apples, brown sugar and butter in a buttered 1½-quart baking dish. Sprinkle with salt. Repeat the layers.

Bake, covered, at 350 degrees for 30 minutes. Bake, uncovered, for 30 minutes longer or until the apples are tender.

Serves Four

Ingredients
2 medium sweet potatoes
    or yams
1½ cups thinly sliced
    peeled tart apples
½ cup packed brown sugar
¼ cup butter
salt to taste

Spaghetti Squash Parmesan

Fry the bacon in a skillet until crisp. Drain the bacon and crumble.

Score the squash ½ inch deep in 2 places. Place on a baking sheet. Bake at 350 degrees for 30 minutes. Cut into halves lengthwise and discard the seeds. Scrape the spaghetti-like strands away from the sides of the squash with a fork.

Place the squash on a baking sheet. Sprinkle with the salt and pepper and dot with butter. Sprinkle with the cheese and bacon. Broil for 5 minutes. Scrape the strands into a bowl to serve.

Serves Four

Ingredients
8 slices bacon
1 large spaghetti squash
½ teaspoon salt
¼ teaspoon pepper
¼ cup butter
¾ cup grated Parmesan
    cheese

Fall squash are among the most beautiful vegetables of the year. From their gorgeous colors and naturally striped patterns to their versatility, they're a treat. Plus, they keep for weeks. Choose squash that are heavy for their size and have no soft spots. Most squash require a heavy sharp knife or cleaver for slicing, so you might look for pre-sliced, seeded, and tightly wrapped squash in the produce section. These should be refrigerated and used fairly soon. For the simplest preparation, just brush the cut edge with olive oil, sprinkle with salt and pepper, and bake until tender.

Remove the kernels from the cobs easily for this vegetable medley by slicing off one end of the corn to stand it upright. Steady it with one hand at the top and slice from top to bottom with a super-sharp serrated knife.

Navajo Vegetable Medley

Ingredients

1 medium onion, chopped
1 clove of garlic, chopped
2 tablespoons margarine or
    bacon drippings
kernels of 3 ears of sweet
    corn, or 1 (16-ounce) can
    corn, drained
3 medium tomatoes,
    chopped
3 medium zucchini, sliced
    1/4 inch thick
2 teaspoons sugar
1/4 teaspoon (or more)
    cumin
1 teaspoon salt
1/4 teaspoon pepper

Sauté the onion and garlic in the margarine in a medium saucepan over medium heat until tender. Add the corn, tomatoes, zucchini, sugar, cumin, salt and pepper and mix well. Bring to a boil and reduce the heat. Simmer, covered, for 10 to 15 minutes or until the vegetables are tender. Serve warm.

Serves Ten

Herbed Rice

Ingredients

3 tablespoons minced
    onion
1 tablespoon minced garlic
1/4 cup butter
2 cups uncooked white rice
2 bay leaves
1 teaspoon chopped fresh
    marjoram
1 teaspoon chopped fresh
    basil
1 teaspoon chopped fresh
    thyme
4 cups chicken broth

Sauté the onion and garlic in the butter in a saucepan until tender but not brown. Add the rice, bay leaves, marjoram, basil and thyme. Stir in the chicken broth. Simmer, covered, for 25 minutes or until the liquid is absorbed. Discard the bay leaves.

Serves Ten

Applesauce bread can be made a month in advance and frozen for holiday giving. It stays very moist because of the applesauce, and slices easily.

Utah Valley Applesauce Bread

Mix the flour, cornstarch, sugar, baking soda, cinnamon, cloves, allspice, nutmeg and salt in a bowl.

Combine the oil, applesauce, raisins and pecans in a bowl. Add to the dry ingredients and mix well.

Spoon into 2 greased 5x9-inch loaf pans or 5 small loaf pans. Bake large loaves at 350 degrees for 1 hour. Bake smaller loaves for 30 minutes. Cool in the pans for several minutes; remove to wire racks to cool completely.

Makes Two Large Loaves or Five Small Loaves

Ingredients
4 cups flour
2 tablespoons cornstarch
2 cups sugar
4 teaspoons baking soda
1 teaspoon cinnamon
$1/2$ teaspoon cloves
$1/2$ teaspoon allspice
$1/2$ teaspoon nutmeg
$1/2$ teaspoon salt
1 cup vegetable oil
3 cups applesauce
1 cup raisins
$1/2$ cup chopped pecans

Soda bread is wonderful warm, spread with butter, as an accompaniment to soup, and great the next day toasted.

Brown Soda Bread

Ingredients

1³/₄ cups all-purpose flour
1³/₄ cups whole wheat flour
3 tablespoons toasted
    wheat bran
3 tablespoons toasted
    wheat germ
2 tablespoons rolled oats
2 tablespoons dark brown
    sugar
1 teaspoon baking soda
¹/₂ teaspoon salt
2 tablespoons chilled
    butter, chopped
2 cups (about) buttermilk

Mix the all-purpose flour, whole wheat flour, wheat bran, wheat germ, oats, brown sugar, baking soda and salt in a large bowl. Add the butter and rub in with the fingertips until the mixture has the texture of fine cornmeal. Add enough buttermilk to form a soft dough, mixing well.

Place in a buttered 5x9-inch loaf pan. Bake at 425 degrees for 40 minutes or until the bread is dark brown and a tester inserted in the center comes out clean. Remove to a wire rack to cool completely.

Makes One Loaf

Danish Coffee Cakes

For the filling, combine the milk, egg yolk, sugar, flour, vanilla and salt in a saucepan and mix well. Cook until thickened, stirring constantly. Let stand, covered, until cool.

For the topping, combine the butter, sugar and nuts in a bowl and mix well.

For the coffee cake, combine the margarine and 3/4 cup sugar in a large mixer bowl. Microwave the milk in a microwave-safe bowl until lukewarm. Pour over the margarine and sugar and let stand until the margarine melts.

Dissolve the yeast and 1 tablespoon sugar in the lukewarm water in a small bowl; let stand for 5 minutes. Add to the margarine mixture with the eggs and mix well. Add the flour and salt gradually, mixing with a dough hook until smooth. Place in a greased large bowl, turning to coat the surface. Let rise in a warm place for 1 1/2 hours.

Punch the dough down and divide into 3 equal portions. Pat each into a large rectangle on a baking sheet. Spoon the filling down the center third of each rectangle.

Cut the outer thirds of each rectangle into strips, cutting to the filling. Fold in the ends and cross the pastry strips over the filling in a braided effect. Let rise until doubled in bulk. Brush with the egg white and sprinkle with the topping mixture. Arrange cherries over the top. Bake at 375 degrees for 20 minutes.

To substitute *Almond Filling* for Cream Filling, combine 1/4 cup butter, 3/4 cup sugar, 1/3 cup rolled oats and 2 teaspoons almond extract in a bowl and mix well.

Makes Three Coffee Cakes; Each Serves Six

Cream Filling
1 cup milk
1 egg yolk
1/3 cup sugar
3 tablespoons flour
1 teaspoon vanilla extract
1/4 teaspoon salt

Crumb Topping
1/4 cup butter
1/2 cup sugar
1/4 cup chopped nuts

Coffee Cake
1 cup margarine
3/4 cup sugar
2 cups milk
2 envelopes dry yeast
1 tablespoon sugar
1/2 cup lukewarm water
2 eggs
6 cups (about) flour
1 teaspoon salt
1 egg white, lightly beaten
maraschino cherries

Morning Glory Muffins make a great take-along breakfast.
They're easy to eat in the car, too.

Morning Glory Muffins

Ingredients
6 eggs
2 cups vegetable oil
4 teaspoons vanilla extract
4 cups flour
2½ cups sugar
4 teaspoons baking soda
4 teaspoons cinnamon
1 teaspoon salt
4 cups grated carrots
1 cup raisins
1 cup flaked coconut
2 apples, peeled, grated
1 cup chopped pecans

Beat the eggs in a mixer bowl until smooth. Add the oil and vanilla and mix well.

Sift the flour, sugar, baking soda, cinnamon and salt together. Add to the egg mixture and mix just until moist. Stir in the carrots, raisins, coconut, apples and pecans.

Spoon into oiled muffin cups. Bake at 350 degrees for 15 minutes or until the tops spring back when lightly touched. Cool in the pans for 5 minutes. Remove to a wire rack to cool completely.

Makes Three Dozen

Autumn

Caramelized Walnuts

Beat the whipping cream in a mixer bowl until frothy. Add the sugar gradually, beating constantly until soft peaks form. Spoon into 6 dessert glasses.

Heat the honey in a heavy skillet over medium heat until it begins to foam. Add the walnuts. Cook until the honey is dark golden brown, stirring with a wooden spoon. Spoon over the whipped cream in stemmed goblets or small serving glasses. Garnish with mint, orange zest or candied flowers. Serve immediately.

Serves Six

Ingredients
1 cup heavy whipping
   cream
1 tablespoon sugar
3 tablespoons honey
2 cups walnut halves

Garnish
mint, orange zest or
   candied flowers

Irresistible Honey Corn

Combine the butter, cream, sugar and honey in a 6-quart saucepan. Cook to 234 degrees on a candy thermometer, soft-ball stage. Pour over the popcorn in a large bowl and mix to coat well.

Serves Twenty to Thirty

Ingredients
1 cup butter
1 cup heavy cream
4 cups sugar
1 cup honey
3 (16-ounce) bags
   pre-popped buttered
   popcorn

Utah is known as the Beehive State because Brigham Young, leader of the Mormon pioneers, chose the beehive as the symbol to denote the industrious workers of "the State of Deseret." Along with bread, cheese, wine, and beer, honey is one of the most ancient of culinary treasures and, when made with care, each imparts the character of the land in which its main ingredients grow. In Utah the flavor comes from acres of alfalfa and clover, both of which result in a pleasingly mild honey. True aficionados can taste the difference, and once they have Utah honey, no other source will do. Salt Lake's Red Rock Brewing Company uses it in their distinctive Honey Wheat Beer.

Berry Lemon Mousse

Ingredients

1 envelope unflavored
   gelatin
$^3/_4$ cup lemon juice
6 egg yolks, at room
   temperature
$^3/_4$ cup sugar
3 tablespoons butter
1 (10-ounce) package
   frozen raspberries in
   syrup, thawed
6 egg whites, at room
   temperature
$^1/_4$ teaspoon salt
$^1/_4$ cup sugar
$^3/_4$ cup whipping cream,
   whipped
$1^1/_2$ cups fresh raspberries
sugar to taste

Soften the gelatin in $^1/_4$ cup of the lemon juice in a small bowl for 5 minutes.

Combine the remaining $^1/_2$ cup lemon juice with the egg yolks, $^3/_4$ cup sugar and butter in a medium saucepan. Cook over medium heat until the mixture coats the back of a metal spoon, stirring constantly. Add the gelatin mixture and stir for 1 minute or until dissolved. Spoon into a large bowl. Chill until the mixture mounds, stirring frequently.

Press the raspberries through a fine sieve into a small bowl; measure $^1/_3$ cup purée and set aside.

Beat the egg whites with the salt until soft peaks form. Add $^1/_4$ cup sugar 2 tablespoons at a time, beating constantly until the egg whites are glossy and firm.

Stir $^1/_3$ cup of the beaten egg whites into the chilled mixture. Fold in the remaining beaten egg whites and whipped cream gently.

Spoon half the mixture into a clear dish. Dollop half the reserved raspberry purée by teaspoonfuls in 6 or 7 places over the top. Cut through the layers with the flat edge of a dinner knife to marbleize lightly. Repeat with the remaining lemon mixture and raspberry purée.

Chill, covered, for 2 hours or until set. Combine the fresh raspberries with sugar to taste. Serve with the mousse.

Serves Six

If you want to serve up something elegant for dessert, this is it. The elements may be prepared ahead of time and assembled just before serving.

Chocolate Pears in Raspberry Sauce

For the chocolate sauce, combine the sugar and baking cocoa in a saucepan and mix well. Stir in the water and corn syrup until smooth. Bring to a boil over medium heat, stirring constantly. Remove from the heat and stir in the vanilla. Pour into a bowl and cover; chill until serving time.

For the raspberry sauce, combine the raspberries and sugar in a saucepan. Cook over medium-low heat for 3 minutes or until the sugar dissolves, stirring constantly. Strain the mixture and return to the saucepan. Stir in the cornstarch. Bring to a boil over medium heat. Boil for 1 minute or until slightly thickened. Pour into a bowl and cover. Chill until serving time.

For the pears, slice 1/4 inch from the bottom of each pear to make it stand upright. Peel and core from the bottom, leaving the stem intact.

Bring the water, lemon juice and vanilla bean to a boil in a heavy saucepan over medium heat. Stand the pears in the liquid and reduce the heat. Simmer, covered, for 20 minutes or until the pears are tender. Remove from the liquid and cool.

To serve, place 1 tablespoon raspberry sauce on each dessert plate. Stand 1 pear in the raspberry sauce and drizzle with 1 tablespoon of the chocolate sauce.

Serves Six

Chocolate Sauce
2 1/2 tablespoons sugar
2 1/2 tablespoons unsweetened baking cocoa
2 tablespoons water
2 tablespoons light corn syrup
1/2 teaspoon vanilla extract

Raspberry Sauce
1 1/4 cups frozen unsweetened raspberries, thawed
2 1/2 tablespoons sugar
1/2 teaspoon cornstarch

Pears
6 ripe pears
3 cups water
3 tablespoons lemon juice
1/2 large vanilla bean, split

Pumpkin Squares with Dates and Pecans

Ingredients

1 cup plus 2 tablespoons
    unsalted butter, softened
2 cups packed brown sugar
2 large eggs
1 cup solid-pack canned
    pumpkin
1 teaspoon vanilla extract
1/4 cup water
2 1/2 cups flour
1 1/2 teaspoons baking
    powder
3/4 teaspoon cinnamon
1/2 teaspoon freshly grated
    nutmeg
1/2 teaspoon ground cloves
1/2 teaspoon salt
1 pound pitted dates, cut
    into thirds
1 1/2 cups chopped pecans

Cream the butter and brown sugar in a mixer bowl until light and fluffy. Beat in the eggs 1 at a time. Add the pumpkin, vanilla and water and mix well.

Sift the flour, baking powder, cinnamon, nutmeg, cloves and salt together. Toss the dates with 1/2 cup of the flour mixture to coat well. Add the remaining flour mixture to the pumpkin mixture gradually, mixing at low speed. Stir in the dates and pecans.

Spoon into a greased 9x13-inch baking pan. Bake on the center oven rack at 350 degrees for 1 hour or until a tester inserted in the center comes out clean. Cool in the pan on a wire rack. Cut into squares and serve with vanilla ice cream.

Serves Twelve

Ras-Pearie Pie

For the pastry, mix the flour and salt in a bowl. Cut in the shortening until the mixture has the texture of fine crumbs. Add the ice water and mix to form a dough. Divide the pastry into 2 portions. Roll 1 portion to fit into an 11-inch pie plate and place in the plate.

For the filling, combine the pears, 2/3 cup sugar, lemon juice and 3 tablespoons tapioca in a bowl. Combine the raspberries, 2/3 cup sugar and 2 tablespoons tapioca in a bowl.

Spoon the raspberry mixture into the prepared plate. Spoon the pear filling over the raspberries. Dot with the butter. Roll the remaining pastry portion and place over the filling. Trim and flute the edges. Brush the top pastry with the beaten egg and cut vents.

Bake at 350 degrees for 50 to 60 minutes or until the crust is golden brown. Cool to room temperature.

Serves Eight

Pastry
2²/₃ cups flour
1 teaspoon salt
1 cup butter-flavor
   shortening
10 tablespoons ice water
1 egg, beaten

Filling
6 cups sliced peeled pears
2/3 cup sugar
3 tablespoons lemon juice
3 tablespoons tapioca
3 cups fresh raspberries
2/3 cup sugar
2 tablespoons tapioca
2 tablespoons butter

Half of Bear Lake sits in Utah, the other half in Idaho to the north. Berries from the second, or autumn, crop from this region are prized for their intense sweet flavor. Capture the flavor any way you can!

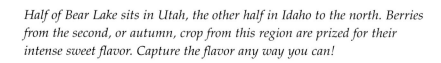

Make a batch to take along on a hike or camping trip. Golden raisins and regular dark raisins are good energy boosters.

Goblin Valley Raisin Cookies

Ingredients
2 cups golden raisins
1 cup water
1 cup vegetable oil
1½ cups sugar
2 eggs, beaten
1 teaspoon vanilla extract
3 cups flour
1 teaspoon baking soda
½ teaspoon salt
sugar

Bring the raisins to a boil in the water in a small saucepan and boil until the water is absorbed.

Beat the oil and 1½ cups sugar in a mixer bowl for 2 minutes. Beat in the eggs and vanilla. Mix the flour, baking soda and salt and add to the oil mixture; mix well. Stir in the raisins; the dough will be sticky.

Chill the dough for 15 to 20 minutes. Shape into 1¼-inch balls and roll in additional sugar. Place 2 inches apart on ungreased cookie sheets.

Bake at 350 degrees for 12 to 15 minutes or until golden brown. Cool on the cookie sheets for several minutes; remove to a wire rack to cool completely. Store in an airtight container.

Makes Four Dozen

Autumn

Goblin Valley State Park is a spooky, spectacular wonder of nature, populated by thousands of intricately eroded rock "creatures." Trails north and west of the park may lead through stream narrows barely wide enough to squeeze through with a backpack. The park is located between Green River and Hanksville, in the southeast quarter of the state.

Color Country Cocktail

Pour the boiling water over the tea bags in a saucepan; steep for 5 minutes. Remove and discard the tea bags.

Add the orange juice, cranberry juice, honey, cinnamon stick and cranberries to the saucepan. Bring just to a boil and reduce the heat. Simmer for 15 minutes. Stir in the liqueur. Strain into mugs to serve.

Serves Eight

Ingredients
6 cups boiling water
4 orange spice tea bags
2 cups orange juice
1 quart cranberry juice
2 tablespoons honey
1 (2-inch) cinnamon stick
1/2 cup fresh cranberries
1 1/2 cups orange liqueur

Marmalade Hill Cider

Combine the apple cider, brown sugar, lemon juice, allspice, cloves, cinnamon sticks and nutmeg in a saucepan. Bring to a boil and reduce the heat. Simmer for 5 minutes. Strain into mugs to serve.

Serves Six

Ingredients
4 1/2 cups apple cider
1 tablespoon light brown
  sugar
3 tablespoons fresh lemon
  juice
25 whole allspice
12 whole cloves
3 cinnamon sticks
1/4 teaspoon freshly grated
  nutmeg

Fresh-pressed Utah apple cider makes the season complete. It's always for sale at farmers' markets, but you can also find it in better food stores. Marmalade Hill, named for the fruit orchards that used to dot the landscape, is a charming residential historic district, just west of the state capitol in Salt Lake City. Its narrow winding streets reveal homes with great architectural details, as well as several famous polygamists' homes from the old days.

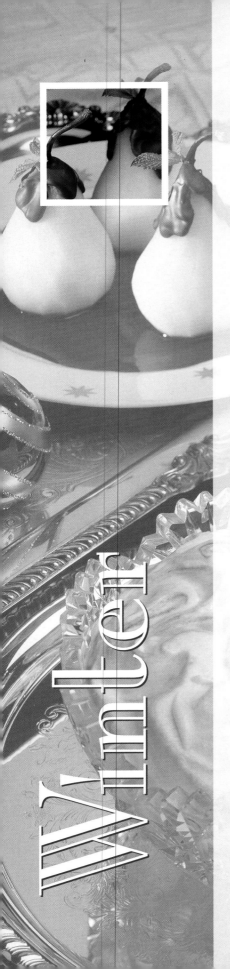

Utah winters are famous for one thing. It's white and it's deep. Among powder skiers, it is legendary. It's our uniquely dry snow, of course. When moisture-laden clouds blow east from the Pacific, they float across the desert, which "bakes" much of the moisture out. When those clouds bump up against the towering Rocky Mountains, the remaining precipitation rapidly cools and, down below, the ski resorts welcome the snow with wide, open runs and challenging vertical drops.

It's hard to believe there was a time when Utah skiing was considered an insider's secret. But long before Salt Lake City won the bid to host the 2002 Winter Olympics, word was out. Our magical combination of challenging alpine slopes, powdery snow, and world-class facilities draws skiers from every country to Utah's fourteen downhill and seven cross-country areas.

Daily air shipments of seafood and produce provide sparkling fresh ingredients through the winter. While we are lucky to have access to almost every exotic item imaginable, it's often the traditional in-season items such as bright pink grapefruit and tart cranberries that we treasure. And speaking of tradition, who doesn't love a hearty portion of herb-laced mashed potatoes after a day on the slopes? Paired with juicy pork tenderloin, they make a meal to satisfy any high-altitude, sports-induced appetite. As for casual entertaining, this is the season to revel in everything from snow picnics to fireside suppers, complete with steaming bowls of chili or soup. For something a little more elegant, a lavish dessert buffet is always a welcome idea after an evening at the ballet or theater.

Fresh Cranberry Relish

Cranberries and the holidays always go together, but you don't have to limit the tart berries to those special days. When fresh berries are in the market, buy a few extra bags to keep in the freezer for the rest of winter.

This cranberry relish recipe makes a wonderful accompaniment to turkey and roast pork. It's also as beautiful as it is tasty spread over a round of soft Brie. It's good as a jam on rolls—and don't forget cranberry relish on sandwiches. The relish needs to sit for four days for the best flavor, so plan ahead.

  1 pound cranberries
  2 oranges
  4 apples
  2 cups sugar

Wash and sort the cranberries. Grate 1 tablespoon zest from the oranges, then peel away all the remaining white pith. Slice the oranges, discarding the seeds. Peel, core and slice the apples. Combine the fruit with the orange zest and sugar in a food processor or blender. Process until ground. Place in an airtight container and chill in the refrigerator for 4 days or longer.

Winter Essentials

Winter Essentials

Mashed Potatoes

The best mashed potatoes come from potatoes with the highest starch content—usually russets (a.k.a. Idahos) or white potatoes. Some people like them whipped up to a smooth silky consistency. Others adore a more rustic style, with a few lumps and sometimes the potato skins. If you really want a silky smooth consistency, use a hand cranked food mill, or an inexpensive potato ricer—a tool that pushes the cooked potatoes through a sieve-like basket. You'll get a less smooth rendition with a handheld potato masher and an electric beater. Either way, you can vary the liquids you whip with the potatoes as noted in this basic recipe. Start with 1/2 cup liquid and add more if needed.

2 pounds (6 medium) potatoes
4 cups water
1/2 cup (or more) half-and-half
1/4 cup butter or olive oil
1/2 teaspoon salt

Peel the potatoes or leave the skins on as desired; cut into quarters. Boil in the water in a saucepan until tender; drain. Mash in a large bowl with a hand-held masher or put through a food mill or ricer. Add the half-and-half, butter and salt and beat with a hand mixer until of the desired consistency.

For *Southwest Mashed Potatoes*, cook the potatoes with garlic, and stir in roasted poblano chiles, sautéed onions and cilantro.

Other variations include substituting sweet potatoes or yams, celery root, turnips, rutabagas or parsnips for half the potatoes. Substitutions for the half-and-half include low-fat milk, buttermilk, chicken broth or the reserved cooking water. Additions include cloves of garlic, freshly chopped dill, chives, flat-leaf parsley, basil, horseradish or grated Parmesan cheese.

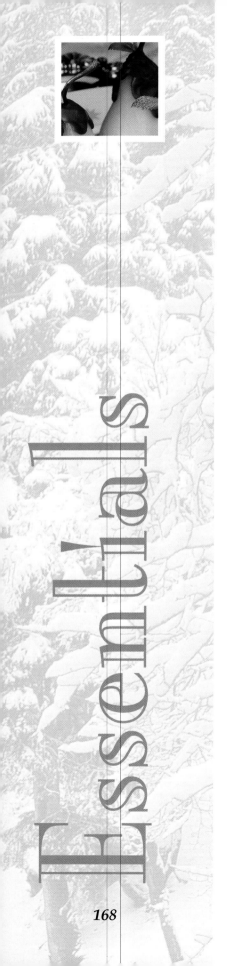

Roasted Garlic

When garlic is roasted, it takes on a whole new character—soft, milky, and nutty tasting. It becomes so creamy you can squeeze it out of its thin skin. This soft garlic makes a wonderful spread for smearing on thick slices of crusty bread, toasted thin-sliced baguettes, or vegetables. You can also rub it between the skin and meat of chicken for roasting, or whip it into mashed potatoes.

> 1 head garlic
> 1 tablespoon olive oil

Place the head of garlic on a square of foil large enough to wrap it completely. Fan out a few of the garlic cloves and drizzle the entire head with the olive oil. Seal the foil. Bake at 450 degrees for 45 minutes or until soft and tender. Let stand just until it is cool enough to handle and serve warm.

Essentials

Winter
Essentials

Winter Essentials

Classic Swiss Fondue

Make sure to use thick, substantial bread cubes for this delicious fondue, or serve it with slices of crisp apples and winter pears for a delicious contrast to the bread. Dig in the minute the fondue is ready.

3 tablespoons butter
3 tablespoons flour
1 teaspoon dry mustard
freshly ground pepper to taste
1 cup milk
2 cups chopped Cheddar cheese
French bread, cubed
sliced crisp apples and pears
steamed broccoli and cauliflower

Melt the butter in a saucepan over medium heat. Stir in the flour, dry mustard and pepper. Cook for 1 minute and remove from the heat. Stir in the milk gradually. Bring to a boil over medium heat, stirring constantly until thickened. Stir in the cheese until melted. Spoon into a fondue pot and serve with bread, fruit or vegetables.

Come For Dessert

Lemon Berry Mousse
Chocolate Pears in Raspberry Sauce
Picture-Perfect Macaroons
Raspberry Fingers
Chocolate-Covered Strawberries
Ginger Lemon Tea
Snow-Capped Hot Chocolate

Cozy Fireside Dinner

Tony Caputo's Red Pesto
Tomato and Broccoli Salad
Market Street Meatloaf
Grapevine's Potato Pie
Date Crumb Bars
Maple Mousse
Apple Cider
Squatters Beehive Lager

Menus

Winter Menus

This elegant holiday appetizer may also be made with small wheels of Brie. The rind of perfectly ripe Brie should look and feel plump, as though the creamy cheese inside just can't wait to ooze out. Pale brown edges around the rind also indicate ripeness.

Cranberry-Glazed Brie

Ingredients
3 cups cranberries
$^1/_3$ cup dried currants
$^3/_4$ cup packed brown sugar
$^1/_3$ cup water
$^1/_8$ teaspoon dry mustard
$^1/_8$ teaspoon allspice
$^1/_8$ teaspoon ground cloves
$^1/_8$ teaspoon ground ginger
$^1/_8$ teaspoon ground
  cardamom
1 (8-inch) wheel Brie

Combine the cranberries, currants, brown sugar, water, dry mustard, allspice, cloves, ginger and cardamom in a heavy nonaluminum saucepan. Cook over medium heat for 5 minutes or until most of the cranberries pop, stirring frequently. Cool to room temperature. Chill in the refrigerator for up to 1 week at this point if desired.

Cut away the top rind of the cheese, leaving a 1-inch border. Place on a foil-lined baking sheet. Spread with the cranberry mixture. Chill, covered, for 12 hours at this point if desired. Bring to room temperature before baking.

Bake the cheese at 350 degrees for 12 minutes or until soft. Serve warm or at room temperature with fruit slices and crackers.

Serves Fifteen

Winter

Phyllo Pesto Pizza

Thaw the phyllo for 5 hours or longer. Spray a baking sheet with nonstick cooking spray. Unroll the phyllo sheets and cut the stacked layers into halves. Layer 6 sheets of the pastry on the baking sheet, spraying each sheet with the cooking spray. Cover with a slightly damp towel. Return the unused phyllo to the refrigerator.

Sauté the mushroom in the olive oil in a skillet until tender; drain and chop the mushroom. Drain the artichokes on a paper towel, patting to absorb excess moisture. Drain any accumulated olive oil off the top of the pesto.

Spread the pesto carefully over the phyllo. Sprinkle with the artichokes, mushroom, bell pepper and black olives. Top with the Parmesan cheese.

Bake the pizza at 375 degrees for 10 to 15 minutes or until the phyllo is crisp. Cut into squares and serve warm.

Serves Ten

Ingredients

1 package frozen phyllo dough
1 portobello mushroom
1 tablespoon olive oil
1 (9-ounce) jar artichoke hearts
1 (6-ounce) jar prepared pesto
1 red bell pepper, chopped
3/4 cup sliced black olives
3/4 cup grated Parmesan cheese

Phyllo is a staple for Utah's large Greek population—and for anyone who has become friendly with the versatility of this paper-thin pastry. You can buy it in every Greek delicatessen, of course, and it's usually available in the frozen food section of most supermarkets. Thaw it in the refrigerator overnight. Unopened, it will keep in the refrigerator for up to one month. Work with the minimum number of phyllo sheets at a time, keeping the remaining sheets covered with a damp towel as they dry and crack very quickly when exposed to air. But don't be intimidated by phyllo's fragile nature. It is forgiving. If it breaks, patch it with melted butter, using a good-quality soft pastry brush.

Hot Sausage Dip

Brown the sausage in a large skillet, stirring until crumbly. Add the jalapeño peppers, green chiles, onion, bell pepper and tomato. Cook for 10 to 15 minutes or until tender and of the desired consistency.

Combine with the cream cheese and sour cream in a large saucepan or slow cooker. Simmer or cook on Low for several hours or until ready to serve. The dip becomes hotter the longer the flavors blend.

Serves Twenty-Four

Ingredients
3 pounds hot sausage
1 (7-ounce) can chopped jalapeño peppers, drained
2 large cans chopped green chiles
1 large onion, chopped
1 large bell pepper, chopped
1 large tomato, chopped
3 pounds cream cheese
2 cups sour cream

Tony Caputo's Red Pesto

Soften the sun-dried tomatoes in boiling water for 1 minute. Drain and pat dry. Combine with the olive oil, Parmesan cheese, parsley and garlic in a food processor and process until smooth. Serve with fresh bread or toasted baguette slices.

Serves Sixteen

Ingredients
3 ounces sun-dried tomatoes
3/4 cup (or more) extra-virgin olive oil
1/4 cup grated Parmesan cheese
1 cup packed fresh parsley
4 cloves of garlic

Tony Caputo, a respected and well-known Italian food lover, merchant and caterer, is one of the owners of Tony Caputo's Deli and Market. The huge sunny loft-type space is set in an old Firestone Tire building, across the street from Pioneer Park in the recently revitalized west side of downtown Salt Lake City. Its shelves are packed with all kinds of pastas, condiments, and sauces, and its deli cases are treasure troves of cured meats, cheeses, olives, and so much more. Tony shared his special recipe for red pesto with us and recommends spreading it on thin-sliced toasted baguette slices.

After-Ski Minestrone

Sauté the prosciutto and onion in the heated olive oil in a large saucepan until the onion is tender. Add the garlic and sauté for 1 minute. Add the celery, carrot and green beans. Sauté for 3 minutes.

Add the tomatoes, chicken broth and oregano. Bring to a boil and reduce the heat. Simmer, covered, for 20 minutes or until the vegetables are tender.

Stir in the lima beans, orzo and rosemary. Cook for 15 minutes longer. Discard the rosemary. Add the Parmesan cheese and season with salt and pepper.

Serves Five or Six

Ingredients
4 ounces prosciutto, chopped
1 medium onion, chopped
2 tablespoons olive oil
4 cloves of garlic, chopped
1/2 cup chopped celery
1/2 cup grated carrot
1 cup (medium pieces) fresh green beans
2 cups canned peeled tomatoes
9 cups chicken broth
1/2 teaspoon oregano
1 cup mashed cooked lima beans or cannellini beans
1/2 cup uncooked orzo
1 rosemary sprig
1/2 cup grated Parmesan cheese
salt and pepper to taste

Smooth coconut milk offsets the heat of the Thai red curry paste in this exotic tasting but easy-to-make soup. The paste is available in most Asian markets and often in larger supermarkets.

Thai Soup with Mussels

Ingredients
1 cup dry white wine
1/2 cup thinly sliced onion
1 teaspoon minced garlic
32 mussels, scrubbed,
    beards removed
3 to 4 teaspoons Thai red
    curry paste
1 (14-ounce) can
    unsweetened regular or
    low-fat coconut milk
1/4 cup slivered fresh basil
    leaves

Combine the wine, onion and garlic in a 5- to 6-quart saucepan and bring to a boil. Add the mussels. Cook, covered, over medium heat for 5 to 7 minutes or until the shells open. Remove the mussels to 4 wide soup bowls with a slotted spoon.

Blend the curry paste with the coconut milk in a small bowl. Stir into the broth in the saucepan. Add the basil. Bring to a simmer. Ladle over the mussels in the soup bowls.

Substitute clams for the mussels and increase cooking time to 8 to 10 minutes if desired.

Serves Four

Broccoli and Leek Bisque

Ingredients
1 cup sliced leeks
1 cup sliced mushrooms
3 tablespoons butter
3 tablespoons flour
3 cups chicken broth
1 cup broccoli florets
1 cup light cream
1 cup shredded sharp
    Cheddar cheese

Sauté the leeks and mushrooms in the butter in a saucepan until tender. Stir in the flour. Cook until bubbly. Add the chicken broth. Cook until thickened, stirring constantly.

Add the broccoli. Simmer for 20 minutes or until the broccoli is tender. Stir in the cream. Add the cheese, stirring until melted, or sprinkle the cheese over individual servings.

Serves Four to Six

Beets and oranges make a classic flavor combination. They go particularly well with sturdy, spicy salad greens, such as arugula and radicchio. Mix red and golden beets for a beautiful presentation.

Anasazi Roasted Beet Salad

For the dressing, combine the orange juice, orange zest, honey, vinegar, Dijon mustard and olive oil in a bowl and whisk until smooth. Season with salt and pepper. Chill until serving time.

For the salad, wrap the beets in foil. Roast at 350 degrees for 1¼ hours or until tender. Cool to room temperature; peel and cut the beets into ¼-inch pieces. Chill for up to 2 days at this point if desired.

Toss the beets with the dressing. Arrange the greens on a large plate. Top with the beets and onion. Serve immediately.

Serves Four

Orange Dressing
¼ cup fresh orange juice
1½ teaspoons finely grated orange zest
1½ teaspoons honey
1½ teaspoons balsamic vinegar
1 teaspoon Dijon mustard
½ teaspoon extra-virgin olive oil
salt and pepper to taste

Salad
3 medium beets
4 cups mixed greens
½ cup thinly sliced red onion

Winter

Ancient Pueblo people, also known as the Anasazi, raised corn in southern Utah from about 1 A.D. until 1300. Many of their food-related tools, such as mortars and pestles and storage baskets, can be found in carefully excavated and preserved villages in such areas as the fascinating Anasazi State Park near Torrey. Every now and then, desert hikers come across something the Ancient Ones left behind, carefully tucked in a niche in the rock.

Tomato and Broccoli Salad

Herbed Vinaigrette
²/₃ cup olive oil
¹/₃ cup tarragon or cider
   vinegar
2 tablespoons water
1 teaspoon lemon juice
1 teaspoon sugar
1 clove of garlic, minced
¹/₂ teaspoon celery seeds
³/₄ teaspoon thyme
¹/₄ teaspoon Italian
   seasoning
¹/₄ teaspoon paprika
¹/₄ teaspoon dry mustard
1 teaspoon salt
¹/₄ teaspoon lemon pepper

Salad
5 cups broccoli florets
3 large tomatoes, cut into
   wedges
³/₄ cup sliced fresh
   mushrooms
3 green onions, chopped

For the vinaigrette, combine the olive oil, vinegar, water, lemon juice and sugar in a jar with a lid. Add the garlic, celery seeds, thyme, Italian seasoning, paprika, dry mustard, salt and lemon pepper. Shake to mix well.

For the salad, cook the broccoli in a small amount of water in a saucepan for 5 minutes or until tender-crisp. Rinse in cold water and drain.

Combine the broccoli, tomatoes, mushrooms and green onions in a large bowl. Add the dressing and mix well. Chill, covered, for 1 hour or longer. Drain to serve or serve with a slotted spoon.

Serves Six to Eight

Honey Mustard Dressing is especially good over a salad of spinach, thinly sliced red onion, orange sections, and crumbled crisp-fried bacon. It is also good with spinach, sliced green apple, toasted walnuts, and crumbled bleu cheese.

Honey Mustard Dressing

Combine the oil, vinegar, honey, Dijon mustard, sesame seeds, garlic and pepper in a jar with a lid and mix well. Store in the refrigerator. Shake well before serving.

Makes One Cup

Ingredients
6 tablespoons salad oil
2 tablespoons cider vinegar
2 tablespoons honey
2 tablespoons Dijon mustard
2 tablespoons toasted sesame seeds
1 clove of garlic, minced
$1/2$ teaspoon freshly ground pepper

Sour Cream Italian Dressing

Combine the mayonnaise, sour cream, milk, honey and vinegar in a bowl. Add the garlic, oregano, basil, salt and pepper and whisk until smooth. Chill, covered, for 2 hours or longer.

Makes One Cup

Ingredients
$1/2$ cup mayonnaise
$1/2$ cup sour cream
2 tablespoons milk
$1/2$ teaspoon honey
1 tablespoon vinegar
1 clove of garlic, minced
$1/2$ teaspoon dried oregano leaves
$1/2$ teaspoon dried basil leaves
$1/4$ teaspoon salt
$1/8$ teaspoon pepper

Ingredients
1 (4-pound) beef tenderloin
1/2 cup butter
2 teaspoons dry mustard
12 ounces mushrooms,
    sliced
1 1/2 cups sliced green
    onions
1 tablespoon lemon juice
1 tablespoon
    Worcestershire sauce
1 teaspoon salt

When sautéing the vegetables for the Sauce Diane, or for other dishes, always let the oil and/or butter heat to sizzling in the skillet before adding the ingredients. Turn down the heat after everything hits the skillet— especially for quick-cooking items, such as minced garlic, shallots, or onions.

Beef Extraordinaire with Sauce Diane

Place the beef on a rack in a baking pan and insert a meat thermometer. Roast at 500 degrees for 30 minutes or until the meat thermometer registers medium for beef.

Heat the butter and dry mustard in a skillet. Add the mushrooms and green onions and sauté for 5 minutes. Add the lemon juice, Worcestershire sauce and salt and cook for 5 minutes longer. Keep warm.

Cut the beef into thick slices. Serve with the sauce and baked wild rice.

Serves Eight

Beef Stroganoff

Cut the beef into ¹/₂x4-inch strips. Heat the butter in a large heavy skillet until the foam subsides. Add the beef and sauté until brown. Add the onions. Cook over medium heat until the onions are tender.

Add the mushrooms, beef broth, nutmeg, basil, salt, cayenne and black pepper. Simmer for 45 minutes or until the beef is tender and the liquid is reduced to about ¹/₂ cup, stirring occasionally.

Blend the cornstarch with the water in a small bowl. Stir into the beef mixture. Simmer for 1 minute, stirring constantly.

Remove the skillet from the heat. Stir in the sour cream. Serve over rice or buttered noodles in a heated serving dish. Garnish with parsley.

Serves Four to Six

Ingredients
2 pounds sirloin steak
2 tablespoons butter
2 large onions, chopped
1 pound mushrooms, sliced
2 cups beef broth
1¹/₄ teaspoons nutmeg
¹/₂ teaspoon dried basil
1¹/₄ teaspoons salt
¹/₄ teaspoon cayenne
¹/₄ teaspoon freshly ground
    pepper
1 tablespoon cornstarch
¹/₄ cup water
²/₃ cup sour cream

Garnish
2 tablespoons chopped
    fresh parsley

Welcome guests to your holiday gathering with ice lanterns lining the walkway to the front door. To make the lanterns, place the openings of balloons around a faucet and fill halfway with water. Blow up the balloon full size and tie a knot. Stand it knot end up in a container and freeze in the freezer, or outside if it is cold enough. Remove the balloon from around the ice to reveal a bowl-shaped lantern. Place a votive candle inside, using an ice pick if necessary to make a hole. Arrange along the walk or drive and light the candles.

If you can't take the time to create your own beef stock for this or other recipes, take heart. Professional chefs and good cooks everywhere recommend Swanson's® beef and chicken broths as the most acceptable canned substitutes.

Stuffed Flank Steak

Ingredients

3 medium onions, chopped

2 cloves of garlic, minced

6 tablespoons (or less) olive oil

¼ cup (or less) butter

1 (4-ounce) can chopped black olives

½ cup chopped cooked ham

1 teaspoon thyme

1 teaspoon salt

1 teaspoon pepper

2 egg yolks, beaten

2 tablespoons minced parsley

1 (2½-pound) flank steak, butterflied

1½ tablespoons butter

2 cups beef stock

Sauté the onions and garlic in the olive oil and ¼ cup butter until tender. Add the olives, ham, thyme, salt and pepper and mix well; remove from the heat. Stir in the egg yolks and parsley.

Spoon the mixture into the center of the butterflied steak. Roll the steak to enclose the filling and tie with string at regular intervals.

Brown the steak roll on all sides in 1½ tablespoons butter in a Dutch oven. Add the beef stock. Braise, covered, in a 300-degree oven for 2 hours.

Remove the steak to a warm serving plate and remove the string carefully. Boil the pan juices until reduced to the desired consistency. Spoon over the steak to serve.

Serves Six

Dead Horse Point in snow
Dead Horse Point State Park

Market Street Meatloaf

Ingredients

¾ cup finely chopped
    onion
¾ cup finely chopped
    scallions
¼ cup finely chopped
    celery
½ cup finely chopped
    carrot
¼ cup minced red bell
    pepper
¼ cup minced green bell
    pepper
2 teaspoons minced garlic
3 tablespoons butter
3 eggs, beaten
1 teaspoon ground cumin
½ teaspoon nutmeg
¼ teaspoon cayenne
salt and freshly ground
    black pepper to taste
½ cup catsup
½ cup half-and-half
2 pounds lean ground beef
12 ounces bulk sausage
¾ cup fresh fine bread
    crumbs

Sauté the onion, scallions, celery, carrot, bell peppers and garlic in the butter in a heavy skillet for 10 minutes or until the vegetables are tender and the moisture has evaporated. Cool to room temperature and chill for 1 hour.

Mix the eggs, cumin, nutmeg, cayenne, salt and black pepper in a bowl and beat until smooth. Beat in the catsup and half-and-half. Add the ground beef, sausage, bread crumbs and chilled sautéed mixture. Mix well with hands for 5 minutes. Shape into a loaf.

Place the meatloaf in a baking dish and place in a large baking pan. Add boiling water to reach halfway up the side of the smaller dish. Bake at 375 degrees for 40 to 60 minutes or until cooked through.

Remove the baking dish from the water and let stand for 20 minutes before serving. Serve with garlic mashed potatoes.

Serves Eight to Ten

Cumin Pork Roast with Wild Mushroom Sauce

For the pork, sprinkle the loin with salt and pepper and rub with the cumin. Place in a roasting pan and insert a meat thermometer. Roast at 375 degrees for 50 minutes or to 150 degrees on the meat thermometer. Remove to a serving platter and tent with foil.

For the sauce, melt 2 tablespoons butter in a medium skillet over medium heat. Add the mushrooms, shallots, garlic and 1 tablespoon jalapeño. Sauté for 15 minutes or until the mushrooms are very tender and begin to brown. Remove from the heat and add the cilantro, oregano, cumin, salt and pepper.

Whisk the flour into the sherry in a medium bowl. Add the chicken broth to the roasting pan, stirring to deglaze. Whisk in the sherry mixture, 1 tablespoon butter and 1 teaspoon jalapeño. Bring to a boil and cook until smooth, whisking constantly. Stir in the mushroom mixture and any accumulated juices from the serving platter. Cook for 5 minutes or until thickened to the desired consistency, stirring occasionally. Adjust the seasonings.

To serve, slice the pork and serve with the sauce. Garnish with cilantro.

Serves Eight

Pork
1 (3¹/₂-pound) center-cut
    pork loin
salt and pepper to taste
1 tablespoon ground cumin

Wild Mushroom Sauce
2 tablespoons butter
8 ounces button
    mushrooms, sliced
4 ounces each oyster and
    shiitake mushrooms,
    sliced
¹/₂ cup chopped shallots
1 clove of garlic, minced
1 tablespoon minced
    jalapeño with seeds
2 tablespoons each finely
    chopped fresh cilantro
    and oregano
1 teaspoon ground cumin
salt and pepper to taste
2 tablespoons flour
¹/₄ cup dry sherry
1 (14-ounce) can chicken
    broth
1 tablespoon butter
1 teaspoon minced jalapeño
    with seeds

Garnish
fresh cilantro

Utah's forests and meadows are strewn with wild mushrooms, but most cooks are happy to find a variety of mushrooms available in local markets. Shiitake mushrooms, in particular, have a robust meaty flavor and texture. When cleaning mushrooms, it's best to wash them lightly and scrub them with a soft fine brush, or to wipe them with a damp paper towel; never soak them in water. They're like sponges, therefore soaking ruins the texture and dilutes the flavor.

*You can put this dish together in a very short time, then let the
roasting aromas fill the house while you forget about dinner for a while.
Substitute 1½ cups homemade or canned chicken broth for
the bouillon cubes and water if you prefer.*

Pork Tenderloin Dinner

Ingredients

2 (1-pound) pork
    tenderloins
1 cup margarine
1 pound fresh mushrooms
1 onion, sliced
2 chicken bouillon cubes
1½ cups water
¼ cup flour
½ cup burgundy or sherry

Brown the pork on all sides in the margarine in a skillet and
remove to a baking dish. Sauté the mushrooms and onion in the
drippings in the skillet.

Dissolve the bouillon cubes in the water in a bowl. Blend in the
flour. Add to the skillet. Cook until thickened, stirring constantly.
Stir in the wine. Pour over the pork.

Bake, covered, at 350 degrees for 1½ hours.

Cut the pork into 2-inch pieces to serve. Serve over rice with
the cooking juices.

Serves Eight to Ten

Sweet Sausage Patties

Ingredients

1 pound lean ground or
    minced pork
¼ cup fresh white bread
    crumbs
2 tablespoons low-fat milk
2 teaspoons maple syrup
2 teaspoons grated orange
    zest
2 teaspoons finely chopped
    flat-leaf parsley
½ teaspoon sweet paprika
½ teaspoon salt
½ teaspoon freshly ground
    pepper

Combine the pork, bread crumbs, milk, syrup, orange zest,
parsley, paprika, salt and pepper in a bowl and mix well. Shape
into 12 patties ½ inch thick and 2 inches in diameter. Chill in the
refrigerator for 1 hour to 2 days at this point to blend flavors
if possible.

Cook in a large nonstick skillet over medium heat for 5
minutes on each side or until cooked through and golden brown.

Serves Six

New Year's Day Brunch

Sauté the mushrooms and onions in $1/2$ cup butter in a skillet until tender. Season with salt and pepper. Brown the sausage in a skillet, stirring until crumbly; drain.

Spread the bread with 2 to 3 tablespoons butter. Arrange half the bread in a shallow baking dish sprayed with nonstick cooking spray. Layer half the mushroom mixture, sausage and cheese over the bread. Repeat the layers.

Combine the eggs, milk, Dijon mustard, dry mustard and nutmeg in a bowl and mix until smooth. Pour over the layers. Chill, covered, in the refrigerator for 8 hours or longer.

Sprinkle with the parsley. Bake, uncovered, at 350 degrees for 1 hour.

Serves Eight to Ten

Ingredients
8 ounces mushrooms, sliced
2 cups thinly sliced onions
$1/2$ cup butter
salt and pepper to taste
$1^{1}/_{2}$ pounds hot sausage
12 slices white bread, crusts trimmed
2 to 3 tablespoons butter, softened
1 pound Cheddar cheese, shredded
5 eggs
$2^{1}/_{2}$ cups milk
1 tablespoon Dijon mustard
1 teaspoon dry mustard
1 teaspoon nutmeg
2 tablespoons chopped parsley

Apple Cider Ham with Mustard

Ingredients
1 (5- to 6-pound) bone-in
    water-added butt ham
3 cups apple cider
1½ cups packed dried
    apples
¾ cup packed light brown
    sugar
6 tablespoons cider vinegar
3 tablespoons Dijon
    mustard

Place the ham in a roasting pan and insert a meat thermometer into the thickest portion. Roast at 325 degrees for 15 minutes per pound or to 150 degrees on the meat thermometer. Cool completely. Chill, covered, for up to 3 days at this point if desired.

Bring the cider and dried apples to a boil in a heavy medium saucepan over medium-high heat. Boil for 8 minutes or until the liquid is reduced to a scant 1½ cups.

Whisk the brown sugar, vinegar and Dijon mustard together in a small bowl. Add to the cider mixture. Simmer for 6 minutes or until reduced to 2¼ cups, stirring occasionally. Chill, covered, for up to 1 day if desired.

Cut eight ½-inch slices from the ham. Overlap the slices in a baking dish. Spoon the sauce over the ham. Bake at 375 degrees for 25 minutes or until the sauce is bubbly. Remove to a serving platter.

Serves Eight

One taste will reveal why this recipe was a winner of the "best chili" contest at the Traveler's Aid Homeless Shelter's annual Chili Affair fund-raiser. You can cook the chicken with the beans, adding it during the last 30 minutes of cooking time.

Chili Blanco

For the chili, rinse and pick the beans and combine with water to cover in a bowl. Soak for 8 to 12 hours; drain. Combine with the onions and chicken broth in a saucepan. Bring to a boil and reduce the heat. Simmer for 1¹/₂ hours.

Add the chicken, green chiles, garlic, oregano, cumin and cayenne. Simmer for 30 to 60 minutes or until of the desired consistency. Remove from the heat. Stir in the sour cream and cheese until melted.

For the dressing, bring the vinegar and sugar to a boil in a saucepan, stirring to dissolve the sugar. Combine the lemon juice, onion powder, paprika, celery seeds and salt in a jar with a lid. Add the vinegar mixture and oil and shake to mix well. Store in the refrigerator for up to 1 week if desired.

For the garnish, combine the desired amount of the dressing with the tomatoes and parsley in a bowl and mix well. Serve with the chili.

Serves Ten to Twelve

Chili
1 pound dried small white navy beans
2 onions, chopped
1 (48-ounce) can chicken broth
4 cups chopped cooked chicken
1 (7-ounce) can chopped green chiles
6 to 8 cloves of garlic, minced
3 tablespoons chopped fresh oregano
4 teaspoons ground cumin
1¹/₂ teaspoons cayenne
1 cup sour cream
3 cups shredded Monterey Jack cheese

Sweet-and-Sour Dressing and Tomato Garnish
¹/₄ cup cider vinegar
¹/₂ cup sugar
juice of 1 lemon
1 teaspoon onion powder
1 teaspoon paprika
2 teaspoons celery seeds
1 teaspoon salt
¹/₃ cup vegetable oil
chopped fresh tomatoes
chopped parsley or cilantro

One of the classics of French cuisine, this savory stew of chicken, red wine, onions, mushrooms, and bacon makes the perfect centerpiece for a casual winter dinner party. Serve it with parslied red potatoes or egg noodles and green peas.

Coq au Vin

Ingredients
3 to 4 ounces lean bacon
2 quarts water
2 tablespoons butter
2¹/₂ to 3 pounds cut-up
    chicken
¹/₂ teaspoon salt, or to taste
¹/₂ teaspoon pepper, or to
    taste
¹/₄ cup cognac
3 cups young, full-bodied
    Beaujolais, Côtes du
    Rhone or Chianti
1 to 2 cups brown chicken
    stock or canned beef
    bouillon
¹/₂ tablespoon tomato paste
2 cloves of garlic, crushed
¹/₄ teaspoon thyme
1 or 2 bay leaves
12 to 24 pearl onions
8 ounces white mushrooms
8 ounces portobello
    mushrooms
3 tablespoons flour
2 tablespoons butter,
    softened

Garnish
parsley

Cut the bacon into ¹/₄x1-inch pieces, discarding the rind. Simmer in the water in a saucepan for 10 to 12 minutes. Drain and rinse in cold water; pat dry. Sauté the bacon in 2 tablespoons heated butter in a heavy 10-inch saucepan or serving casserole until very light brown. Remove with a slotted spoon.

Brown the chicken in the drippings in the saucepan. Season with the salt and pepper. Add the bacon. Cook, covered, for 10 minutes, turning the chicken once. Drain some of the drippings.

Pour in the cognac. Ignite the cognac and shake the saucepan until the flames subside. Add the wine and enough chicken stock to cover the chicken. Stir in the tomato paste, garlic, thyme and bay leaves. Simmer, covered, for 25 to 30 minutes or until the chicken is cooked through; juices will run clear when the chicken is pierced with a knife. Remove the chicken to a platter.

Cook the onions in a nonstick skillet over low heat until golden brown. Add the mushrooms and cook until tender. Keep warm.

Skim the grease from the chicken stock. Increase the heat and boil the stock until it is reduced to about 2¹/₂ cups. Remove from the heat. Adjust the seasonings and discard the bay leaves.

Blend the flour with 2 tablespoons butter in a small bowl. Whisk into the chicken stock. Bring just to a simmer and simmer for 2 to 4 minutes or until the mixture lightly coats a spoon, whisking constantly.

Return the chicken to the saucepan. Simmer just until heated through. Serve from the casserole or remove to a serving platter. Place the mushrooms and onions around the chicken and spoon the sauce over the top. Garnish with parsley.

Serves Six

From the homemade gravy to the pinch of nutmeg, this is great comfort food for any occasion.

Old-Fashioned Chicken Casserole

Mix flour, salt and pepper in a bag. Add the chicken and shake to coat well. Brown a few pieces at a time in the butter in a skillet. Remove to a 3-quart baking dish, reserving the drippings in the skillet.

Add the carrots, potatoes and onions to the baking dish. Pour the chicken broth over the chicken and vegetables and add the thyme. Bake, covered, at 350 degrees for 45 minutes.

Stir 6 tablespoons flour into the reserved drippings, adding additional butter if necessary. Cook for 6 to 8 minutes or until medium brown, stirring constantly. Stir in the milk. Cook until thickened, stirring constantly. Season with salt, pepper and nutmeg.

Pour the gravy over the chicken and vegetables. Bake for 25 to 30 minutes longer. Garnish with parsley.

Serves Eight

Ingredients
flour
salt and pepper
6 tablespoons butter
1 (4- to 5-pound) chicken,
    cut up, or chicken
    breasts
carrots, peeled, chopped
potatoes, peeled, chopped
onions, peeled, chopped
2 cups chicken broth
sprig of thyme
6 tablespoons flour
3 cups milk
salt and pepper to taste
nutmeg to taste

Garnish
parsley

Spicy Chicken and Artichoke Pasta

Ingredients

4 boneless skinless chicken
   breasts
1 clove of garlic, minced
2 tablespoons butter
2 tomatoes, chopped
1 cup sliced mushrooms
1 (4-ounce) jar artichoke
   hearts, drained
2 tablespoons capers
1/4 cup dry red wine
1 cup heavy cream
1/2 teaspoon Tabasco sauce
garlic powder and Cajun
   spice to taste
8 ounces uncooked
   fettucini
3/4 cup grated Parmesan
   cheese

Cut the chicken into bite-size pieces. Sauté the garlic in the butter in a large skillet for several minutes. Add the chicken and sauté until cooked through.

Add the tomatoes, mushrooms, artichoke hearts, capers and wine. Cook over medium heat for 10 minutes. Stir in the cream, Tabasco sauce, garlic powder and Cajun spice. Cook over medium heat for 30 minutes.

Cook the pasta using the package directions; drain. Combine with the chicken and cheese in a serving bowl and toss to mix well.

Serves Four

You can roast four to five red bell peppers for this sauce, or purchase them in a jar at Italian markets and other large food markets.

Phyllo-Wrapped Salmon with Roasted Red Peppers

Purée the red peppers in a food processor or blender.

Layer 2 sheets of phyllo on a work surface, brushing each with butter or spraying with nonstick cooking spray; leave remaining sheets of phyllo covered with plastic wrap or a damp towel until time to use.

Place 1 salmon fillet crosswise on the pastry, 5 inches from the narrow end. Top with 1 tablespoon of the pepper purée. Fold the 5-inch section of pastry over the salmon and fold in the sides. Roll the pastry into a rectangular packet to enclose the salmon. Brush all sides with the butter or spray with the vegetable spray. Repeat with the remaining pastry and salmon.

Place the packets on a baking sheet. Bake at 400 degrees for 35 minutes or until the salmon is cooked through and the pastry is light golden brown. Top with the remaining pepper purée.

Serves Six

Ingredients
1 cup roasted red peppers
12 sheets frozen phyllo pastry, thawed
6 tablespoons melted butter, or nonstick vegetable spray
6 (5-ounce) skinless salmon fillets, 1 inch thick

Mardi Gras Jambalaya

Ingredients
3 ounces bacon, chopped
1/2 cup chopped green
    onions
1 tablespoon flour
1 (14-ounce) can peeled
    chopped tomates
water
1 cup cold cooked rice
1 cup prawns, cooked,
    peeled, deveined
1/8 teaspoon cayenne
salt and black pepper to
    taste

Garnish
2 tablespoons chopped
    parsley

Sauté the bacon in a large skillet over medium heat until the drippings are rendered. Add the green onions. Sauté until the green onions are golden brown.

Stir in the flour. Cook for several minutes. Add the undrained tomatoes and a small amount of water. Cook over medium heat until thickened, stirring constantly.

Stir in the rice and prawns and reduce the heat to low. Cook for 10 minutes, stirring constantly. Season with cayenne, salt and black pepper. Garnish with parsley. Serve with a green salad.

Serves Four

Upton Ramsey, a popular Salt Lake City chef and cooking teacher, says his all-male classes love to prepare and eat this simple jambalaya. The small amount of bacon gives it especially good flavor.

Sautéed Brussels Sprouts with Mustard and Lemon

Trim the Brussels sprouts, discarding outer leaves; cut into halves lengthwise. Add the Brussels sprouts and salt to a saucepan of boiling water. Cook for 2 to 3 minutes or until tender-crisp; drain and cool to room temperature. The recipe can be prepared to this point several hours in advance.

Combine the lemon juice and mustard in a bowl and mix until smooth. Heat the olive oil in a heavy skillet over medium-high heat. Add the Brussels sprouts and sauté for 1 to 2 minutes or until the begin to lightly brown. Add the mustard mixture and season with pepper. Garnish with the lemon curls and serve immediately.

Serves Six to Eight

Ingredients
1 1/2 pounds Brussels
    sprouts
1 teaspoon salt
3 tablespoons lemon juice
1 1/2 tablespoons whole-
    grain mustard
3 tablespoons olive oil
freshly ground pepper
    to taste

Garnish
curls of lemon peel

Cauliflower au Gratin

Remove the leaves from the base of the cauliflower and place it whole in a large saucepan with a small amount of water. Steam, covered, for 10 to 15 minutes or until tender. Remove to a 9x9-inch baking dish.

Toss the bread crumbs with the melted butter in a small bowl; let stand until cool. Add the cheese, salt and pepper and mix well. Spread over the cauliflower.

Bake at 400 degrees for 10 to 15 minutes or until golden brown. Cut into wedges to serve.

Serves Six

Ingredients
1 (1-pound) cauliflower
1/2 cup fresh bread crumbs
1/4 cup melted butter
1/2 cup grated Parmesan
    cheese
salt and pepper to taste

Don't cry over your Onion Tart. To reduce odor and tears, store onions in plastic bags in the refrigerator or place them in the freezer for 15 minutes before slicing.

Onion Tart

Mix the cracker crumbs with ¼ cup melted butter in a bowl. Press over the bottom of a 9-inch tart pan.

Sauté the onions in 2 tablespoons butter in a skillet until tender. Spoon into the prepared tart pan.

Combine the milk, eggs, salt and pepper in a bowl and mix until smooth. Pour over the onions. Sprinkle with the cheese and paprika. Bake at 350 degrees for 30 minutes.

Serves Six to Eight

Ingredients
1 cup saltine cracker
    crumbs
¼ cup melted butter
2 Vidalia or other sweet
    onions, thinly sliced
2 tablespoons butter
¾ cup milk
2 eggs, lightly beaten
¾ teaspoon salt
pepper to taste
¼ cup grated Cheddar
    cheese
paprika to taste

Spinach with Artichokes

Cook the spinach using the package directions; drain well. Add the butter, cream cheese, artichokes, lemon juice, garlic, parsley, salt and pepper and mix well.

Spoon into a baking dish. Bake at 350 degrees for 30 minutes or until bubbly.

Serves Six

Ingredients
2 (10-ounce) packages
    frozen chopped spinach
½ cup butter
8 ounces cream cheese,
    softened
1 (14-ounce) can artichoke
    hearts drained, cut into
    quarters
1½ tablespoons lemon
    juice
1 large clove of garlic,
    minced
¼ cup chopped parsley
salt and pepper to taste

Mountain stream in winter
Big Cottonwood Canyon, Wasatch National Forest

Grapevine's Potato Pie

Ingredients

1 recipe (2-crust) pie pastry

5 ounces smoked bacon, chopped

1½ pounds russet potatoes, peeled, thinly sliced

¼ cup chopped parsley

salt and white pepper to taste

3 tablespoons butter

4 hard-cooked eggs, sliced

½ cup heavy cream

1 egg yolk, beaten

Roll half the pastry on a floured surface and fit into a 9-inch pie plate. Chill the prepared plate and the remaining pastry.

Sauté the bacon in a skillet until brown; drain. Toss the potatoes with the parsley, salt and white pepper in a bowl.

Arrange half the potatoes in an overlapping layer in the pie shell. Sprinkle with the bacon and dot with butter. Arrange the egg slices over the butter and top with the remaining potatoes. Pour the cream over the layers. Chill in the refrigerator.

Roll the remaining pastry and place over the pie. Trim and seal the edge. Brush with egg yolk and cut vents.

Bake at 350 degrees for 20 minutes. Reduce the oven temperature to 300 degrees and bake for 10 to 20 minutes longer or until golden brown.

Serves Eight

Winter

Chef Bill Oblock, of the charming Grapevine Restaurant in Logan, likes the simplicity of this savory pie. Slice the potatoes extra thin for the best flavor and presentation. The city of Logan is located in northern Utah, in the heart of a major dairy region called the Cache Valley. It is also the home of Utah State University, one of the leading agricultural research institutions in the United States.

Pecan Rice

Combine the rice, consommé, water, onion, pimento, mushrooms, butter and pecans in a bowl and mix well. Spoon into a 1½-quart baking dish sprayed with nonstick cooking spray. Bake at 350 degrees for 45 minutes or until the rice is tender and the liquid is absorbed.

Serves Six

Ingredients
¾ cup uncooked long
   grain rice
1⅓ cups beef consommé
½ cup water
1 small onion, chopped
1 (2-ounce) jar chopped
   pimento, drained
1 (4-ounce) can sliced
   mushrooms, drained
¼ cup melted butter
¼ cup chopped pecans

Couscous with Sun-Dried Cranberries

Combine the chicken stock, couscous and cranberries in a saucepan. Bring to a simmer over medium heat and cook using the package directions. Remove from the heat and let stand for 5 minutes. Season with salt and pepper.

Pack the couscous servings into a ½ cup measure and invert onto a serving plate.

Serves Two

Ingredients
8 ounces chicken stock
½ cup uncooked couscous
2 ounces sun-dried
   cranberries or cherries
salt and pepper to taste

Dried fruits, including berries, dates, figs, and raisins, are among the most delectable and versatile items you can keep in the pantry. Their sugars are concentrated, so when you bite into them, your taste buds enjoy a little flavor explosion—the pure essence of the fruit. Enjoy them for a snack, with a platter of winter fruits, a bowl of nuts in the shell, and your favorite cheese; in salads; with steamed rice or couscous; swirled into creamy desserts; baked in muffins; stirred into pancake batter; or whipped up in blender shakes.

Challah

Ingredients
2 cups milk
1/3 cup sugar
6 tablespoons unsalted
   butter
2 envelopes dry yeast
3 eggs, beaten
2 teaspoons salt
6 cups unbleached flour
2 tablespoons unsalted
   butter
1/3 cup cornmeal
1 egg
1 tablespoon cold water
poppy seeds

Bring the milk, sugar and 6 tablespoons butter to a boil in a medium saucepan. Pour into a large bowl and cool to lukewarm, 105 to 115 degrees. Stir in the yeast and let stand for 10 minutes. Stir in the 3 beaten eggs and salt.

Stir in 5 cups of the flour 1 cup at a time to form a sticky dough. Place on a floured surface and knead in enough of the remaining flour to form a smooth and elastic dough.

Place in a bowl buttered with 2 tablespoons butter, turning to coat the surface. Let rise, covered, for 1 1/2 to 2 hours or until tripled in bulk.

Cut the dough into halves on a lightly floured surface. Cut each half into 3 portions. Roll each portion into an 18-inch rope. Braid into 2 loaves and tuck under the ends.

Place well apart on a large baking sheet sprinkled with cornmeal. Let rise, covered, for 1 hour or until nearly doubled in bulk.

Beat 1 egg with 1 tablespoon cold water in a small bowl. Brush over the loaves and sprinkle immediately with poppy seeds. Bake at 350 degrees on the middle oven rack for 30 to 35 minutes or until the loaves are golden brown and sound hollow when tapped. Remove to wire racks to cool. Wrap to store.

Makes Two Large Loaves

Crunchy Whole Wheat Bread

Toast the pine nuts in an 8-inch skillet over medium heat for 4 minutes, shaking frequently. Remove to a small bowl.

Combine the yeast, $1/2$ cup of the water and 1 tablespoon of the honey in a large bowl and let stand for 10 to 15 minutes or until bubbly. Stir in the remaining $1^1/2$ cups water, the remaining honey, the butter and salt.

Add the whole wheat flour, cereal, 1 cup all-purpose flour and the pine nuts and mix well.

Knead in the remaining all-purpose flour on a floured surface for 10 minutes or until smooth and elastic, pressing pine nuts back into the dough. Place in a lightly oiled bowl, turning to coat the surface. Let rise, covered, in a warm place for $1^1/2$ hours or until doubled in bulk.

Knead on a lightly floured surface and divide into halves. Knead each portion until smooth. Place smooth side up well apart on an oiled 12x15-baking sheet. Invert a large bowl over each ball to keep airtight. Let rise for 20 minutes or until slightly puffy.

Bake, uncovered, at 375 degrees for 30 minutes or until brown. Remove to a wire rack. Serve warm or cooled.

Makes Two Loaves

Ingredients
$2/3$ cup pine nuts
1 envelope dry yeast
2 cups (110-degree) water
$1/3$ cup honey
$1/4$ cup butter, softened
1 teaspoon salt
$2^1/2$ cups whole wheat flour
$1/2$ cup wheat and barley
   cereal
3 cups (about) all-purpose
   flour

Millicent Breakfast Cake

Ingredients
2 Texas red grapefruit
1 cup quick-cooking oats
1/2 cup butter or margarine
1 cup sugar
1/2 cup packed brown sugar
2 eggs, beaten
1 1/3 cups flour
1 teaspoon baking soda
1/2 teaspoon cinnamon
vanilla or fruit-flavored
    yogurt

Grate 2 teaspoons peel from the grapefruit. Peel and section the grapefruit over a bowl to catch the juice. Reserve the grapefruit, juice and peel.

Add enough water to the juice to measure 1 1/4 cups. Bring to a boil in a saucepan. Remove from the heat and stir in the oats and butter. Let stand for 20 minutes.

Combine the grapefruit peel, sugar, brown sugar, eggs, flour, baking soda and cinnamon in a large bowl. Stir in the oats mixture. Spoon into a greased 9x13-inch baking pan.

Bake at 350 degrees for 35 minutes. Serve warm or cooled, topped with yogurt and the grapefruit sections.

Serves Ten to Twelve

This delicious breakfast cake is named after a ski lift at Brighton, a long-established family ski resort at the top of Big Cottonwood Canyon. Brighton Ski Resort covers more than 850 acres in the Cache National Forest. Its base elevation is 8,500 feet, while the skiing summit peaks at 10,500 feet. Hard-core skiers will tell you that Brighton offers some of the best back-country access in Utah.

Winter Apricot Soufflés

Pour the boiling water over the apricots in a large bowl. Let stand, covered, for 2 hours.

Butter six 1¼-cup soufflé cups and sprinkle each with ½ teaspoon sugar.

Drain the apricots, reserving 3 tablespoons liquid. Process the apricots with the reserved liquid in a food processor or blender until smooth. Add the amaretto, lemon juice and 1½ tablespoons sugar and process to mix well. Pour into a bowl. Chill for up to 2 days at this point if desired.

Beat the egg whites with the salt and cream of tartar in a large mixer bowl until soft peaks form. Add 1 tablespoon sugar gradually, beating constantly until stiff but not dry peaks form. Fold ¼ of the egg whites into the apricot mixture. Fold in the remaining egg whites ½ at a time.

Spoon into the prepared soufflé cups and place on a baking sheet. Bake at 400 degrees for 20 minutes or until puffed and golden brown. Serve immediately.

Serves Six

Ingredients
2 cups boiling water
1½ cups dried apricots
1 tablespoon sugar
5 teaspoons amaretto
    liqueur
2 teaspoons fresh lemon
    juice
1½ tablespoons sugar
5 large egg whites
pinch of salt
pinch of cream of tartar
1 tablespoon sugar

Cranberry Eggnog Cheesecake

Crust
1½ cups crushed coconut
    bar cookies
6 tablespoons melted butter

Filling
½ cup sugar
2 envelopes unflavored
    gelatin
¼ teaspoon salt
4 egg yolks, lightly beaten
1½ cups eggnog
16 ounces cream cheese,
    softened
1 tablespoon grated orange
    peel
1 teaspoon vanilla extract
4 egg whites
½ teaspoon cream of tartar
½ cup sugar
1 cup whipping cream,
    whipped
1 (16-ounce) can jellied
    cranberry sauce, puréed

For the crust, mix the cookie crumbs and butter in a bowl. Press over the bottom and part way up the side of a 9-inch springform pan. Bake at 350 degrees for 8 to 10 minutes or until golden brown. Cool on a wire rack.

For the filling, combine ½ cup sugar, gelatin and salt in a heavy medium saucepan. Beat the egg yolks with the eggnog in a bowl. Stir gradually into the gelatin mixture. Let stand for several minutes to soften the gelatin.

Cook over low to medium heat until the gelatin dissolves and the mixture thickens slightly, stirring constantly; do not boil. Cool slightly.

Beat the cream cheese, orange peel and vanilla in a mixer bowl until fluffy. Stir in the gelatin mixture until smooth. Chill until the mixture mounds when dropped from a spoon.

Beat the egg whites with the cream of tartar in a mixer bowl. Add ½ cup sugar gradually, beating constantly until stiff, glossy peaks form. Fold the egg whites and whipped cream gently into the chilled mixture.

Spoon ⅓ of the cream cheese mixture into the prepared springform pan. Top with ⅓ of the cranberry puré. Swirl with a spatula to marbleize. Repeat the layering and swirling twice. Chill for 4 hours or longer.

Place the cheesecake on a serving plate. Loosen the side of the pan with a spatula and remove carefully. Chill until serving time.

Serves Eight

This is called a "pop" cake, because the cranberries pop while baking.

Cranberry Pop Cake

For the cake, cream the margarine and sugar in a mixer bowl until light and fluffy. Mix the flour, baking powder and salt in a bowl. Add to the creamed mixture alternately with the evaporated milk, mixing well after each addition. Fold in the cranberries gently to avoid coloring the batter.

Spoon into a greased 8x8-inch cake pan. Bake at 350 degrees for 25 to 30 minutes or until the cake tests done.

For the sauce, combine the butter, sugar and cream in a saucepan. Cook over medium heat until the sugar dissolves. Remove from the heat and stir in the vanilla. Serve hot with the hot cake.

Serves Nine

Cake
3 tablespoons margarine or
   butter, softened
1 cup sugar
2 cups flour
1 tablespoon baking
   powder
1 teaspoon salt
1 cup evaporated milk
2 cups fresh or frozen
   whole cranberries

Butter Sauce
1/2 cup butter
1 cup sugar
3/4 cup whipping cream
1 teaspoon vanilla extract

Date Crumb Bars

Date Filling
1 pound whole pitted dates
²/₃ cup packed light brown
    sugar
²/₃ cup orange juice
1 tablespoon vanilla extract

Crust and Topping
1¹/₂ cups rolled oats
1¹/₂ cups flour
1 cup packed light brown
    sugar
¹/₂ teaspoon baking soda
1 teaspoon cinnamon
salt to taste
1 cup chilled butter, cut
    into pieces
³/₄ cup coarsely chopped
    walnuts

For the filling, combine the dates, brown sugar and orange juice in a medium saucepan. Cook over medium heat until the brown sugar dissolves. Simmer for 3 minutes or until the dates are tender and the syrup is thickened. Cool to room temperature.

Stir in the vanilla. Process the mixture in a food processor until smooth.

For the crust, mix the oats, flour, brown sugar, baking soda, cinnamon and salt in a large bowl. Add the butter and rub in with the fingers until the mixture has the texture of coarse cornmeal and forms moist clumps.

Press half the crumb mixture firmly into the bottom of a buttered 9x13-inch baking pan. Spread the filling in the prepared pan.

For the topping, mix the walnuts with the remaining crumb mixture. Sprinkle it over the filling.

Bake at 350 degrees for 40 minutes or until the topping is golden brown. Cool in the pan on a wire rack. Cut into squares. Serve with vanilla ice cream.

Serves Twelve

Maple Mousse

Soften the gelatin in the water in a small bowl. Combine with the maple syrup, brown sugar and egg yolks in a medium saucepan. Cook over low heat just until the gelatin dissolves and the mixture thickens, whisking constantly. Let stand until slightly thickened.

Beat the egg whites in a small mixer bowl until stiff peaks form. Fold the egg whites and whipped cream gently into the maple syrup mixture.

Spoon into 6 wide-mouth dessert glasses. Chill for 2 hours or until set. Garnish with whipped cream and berries.

Serves Six

Ingredients
1 envelope unflavored
    gelatin
¹/₄ cup water
¹/₂ cup maple syrup
¹/₄ cup packed light brown
    sugar
2 egg yolks
2 egg whites
1 cup whipping cream,
    whipped

Garnish
whipped cream
fresh berries

Kiwifruit Sorbet

Bring the water and sugar to a boil in a heavy saucepan and boil for 5 minutes. Chill in the refrigerator. Stir in the kiwifruit purée and lime juice.

Pour into an ice cream freezer and freeze using the manufacturer's instructions or pour into a freezer container and freeze in the freezer. Store in the freezer for up to 1 month. Let stand at room temperature for 10 minutes before serving.

Serves Four to Six

Ingredients
2 cups water
1 cup (or more) sugar
2 cups kiwifruit purée,
    about 7 to 8 kiwifruit
2 tablespoons lime juice

Dessert menus in some of Utah's favorite restaurants include a selection of brilliantly colored fresh fruit sorbets. The refreshing flavor and texture are especially welcome between courses, or after a rich meal along with a delicate cookie or two. Basically sorbet is like a sweetened fruit "ice" and it never contains milk, as some sherbets, ice cream, and gelatos do. The very best sorbets let the true flavor of the kiwifruit, fresh-squeezed citrus juice, fresh or frozen berries, or very ripe pears or peaches shine through.

Chocolate Lover's Chocolate Chip Cookies

Ingredients
2 cups (12 ounces)
   semisweet chocolate
   chips
4 (1-ounce) squares
   unsweetened chocolate
1/4 cup butter
4 eggs
1 1/3 cups sugar
2 teaspoons vanilla extract
1/2 cup flour
1/2 teaspoon baking powder
1/4 teaspoon salt
2 cups (12 ounces)
   semisweet chocolate
   chips
1 to 3 cups coarsely
   chopped toasted
   walnuts, pecans or
   macadamia nuts

Garnish
melted white chocolate
melted semisweet chocolate

Melt 2 cups chocolate chips, unsweetened chocolate and butter in a heavy saucepan, stirring to blend well. Spoon into a large mixer bowl and cool slightly.

Add the eggs, sugar and vanilla and beat until smooth. Mix the flour, baking powder and salt together. Add to the chocolate mixture and beat at low speed until smooth. Stir in 2 cups chocolate chips and walnuts.

Drop by 1/4 cupfuls 3 inches apart onto a lightly greased cookie sheet; flatten slightly. Bake at 350 degrees for 12 to 15 minutes or until the edges are firm and the surface is dull and cracked. Cool on the cookie sheet for 2 minutes. Remove to a wire rack with a metal spatula to cool completely. Garnish with a drizzle of white chocolate and semisweet chocolate.

Makes Two Dozen

German Gingerbread Cookies

Mix the shortening, butter, molasses and brown sugar in a heavy saucepan. Cook over low heat until the shortening, butter and brown sugar dissolve, stirring to blend well. Remove from the heat.

Sift the flour, baking soda, ginger, cinnamon, cloves and salt into a bowl. Add the molasses mixture and mix well to form a dough. Chill for several hours. Roll 1/8 inch thick on a lightly floured surface and cut as desired. Place on a greased cookie sheet. Bake at 375 degrees for 10 minutes or until the edges are firm. Cool on the cookie sheet for several minutes. Remove to a wire rack to cool completely.

Makes Six Dozen

Ingredients
1/2 cup shortening
1/2 cup butter, softened
1 1/4 cups molasses
3/4 cup packed brown sugar
4 cups flour
1 teaspoon baking soda
2 teaspoons ground ginger
1 teaspoon cinnamon
1 teaspoon ground cloves
1 teaspoon salt

Soft Gingersnaps

Combine the butter and oil in a mixer bowl and beat until smooth. Beat in the egg, 1 cup sugar and molasses. Sift the flour, baking soda, ginger, cinnamon and salt together. Add to the beaten mixture and mix to form a dough.

Roll into 1-inch balls and coat with additional sugar. Place on ungreased cookie sheets. Bake at 350 degrees for 8 to 10 minutes or until puffed. Cool on the cookie sheets for several minutes. Remove to a wire rack to cool completely.

Makes Four Dozen

Ingredients
1/2 cup butter, softened
1/4 cup corn oil
1 egg
1 cup sugar
1/4 cup molasses
2 cups plus 2 tablespoons flour
2 teaspoons baking soda
1 teaspoon ground ginger
1 teaspoon cinnamon
1/2 teaspoon salt
sugar

Raspberry Fingers

Ingredients

1 cup butter, softened
3/4 cup sugar
1 egg
1 teaspoon vanilla extract
2 1/2 cups flour
1/4 teaspoon salt
1 to 2 tablespoons water
raspberry jam

Cream the butter and sugar in a large mixer bowl until light and fluffy. Beat in the egg and vanilla.

Sift the flour and salt together. Add to the creamed mixture 1/3 at a time, mixing well after each addition. Add 1 to 2 tablespoons water if the mixture is too stiff. Shape into a ball and wrap in plastic wrap. Chill for 1 hour.

Cut the dough into 4 portions. Roll each portion into a rope the length of the cookie sheet. Place on a nonstick cookie sheet. Press an indentation down the length of each rope.

Bake at 375 degrees for 10 minutes. Spoon jam into the indentations. Bake for 10 to 12 minutes longer or until golden brown. Cool on the cookie sheet on a wire rack. Slice diagonally.

Makes Three Dozen

Enjoy Snow-Capped Hot Chocolate by the fireside in Utah, or anywhere the snow and rain keep you indoors. Its decadent flavor is reminiscent of the thick blends served in Parisian cafés.

Snow-Capped Hot Chocolate

Melt the chocolate chips in a double boiler over hot water. Stir in the sugar, salt and water. Cook for 10 minutes, stirring constantly. Cool to room temperature.

Beat the whipping cream in a mixer bowl until soft peaks forms. Fold in the cooled chocolate mixture.

To serve, spoon 2 tablespoons of the chocolate mixture into each cup. Fill with the heated milk and stir to blend well.

Serves Eight

Ingredients
1 cup semisweet chocolate
   chips
$1/4$ cup sugar
$1/8$ teaspoon salt
$1/2$ cup boiling water
1 cup whipping cream
1 quart milk, heated

Ginger Lemon Tea

Shave the ginger with a vegetable peeler and measure $1/4$ cup. Combine with the water in a saucepan and bring to a boil. Reduce the heat to low and simmer for 30 minutes.

Strain into a pitcher and add the honey and lemon juice; mix well. Chill in the refrigerator for 8 hours or longer. Serve over ice.

Serves Four

Ingredients
1 fresh gingerroot, peeled
1 quart water
$1/2$ cup honey
$1/2$ cup fresh lemon juice

Utah's Playgrounds

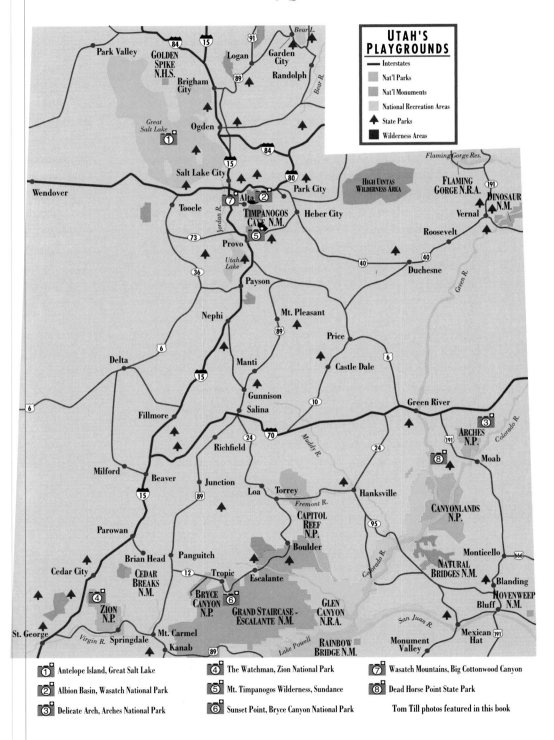

UTAH'S PLAYGROUNDS
- Interstates
- Nat'l Parks
- Nat'l Monuments
- National Recreation Areas
- ▲ State Parks
- Wilderness Areas

1. Antelope Island, Great Salt Lake
2. Albion Basin, Wasatch National Park
3. Delicate Arch, Arches National Park
4. The Watchman, Zion National Park
5. Mt. Timpanogos Wilderness, Sundance
6. Sunset Point, Bryce Canyon National Park
7. Wasatch Mountains, Big Cottonwood Canyon
8. Dead Horse Point State Park

Tom Till photos featured in this book

Herbs

Basil
Member of the mint family with a strong, pungent, peppery flavor reminiscent of licorice and cloves. Popular in Mediterranean cooking, it is the main ingredient in pesto. It is also used in tomato dishes, poultry dishes, soups, and salad dressing.

Bay Leaf
The leaf of the laurel, seldom found fresh in markets. It imparts a lemon-nutmeg flavor and is widely used to flavor soups, stews, vegetables, and meats. Overuse can impart a bitter flavor. It is usually removed before serving.

Bouquet Garni
A French seasoning mix of fresh herbs, usually including parsley, thyme, and bay leaves, in addition to other herbs, spices, or vegetables. It is tied together and used to flavor stews, soups, and sauces.

Chervil
A mild-flavored member of the parsley family with elusive overtones of anise. It is one of the main ingredients in the *fines herbes* traditional to French cooking and is best used fresh.

Chives
A mild-flavored member of the onion family with hollow green stems and purple flowers, all of which are edible. Available fresh, dried, or frozen, chives should be added to cooked dishes toward the end of the cooking time to retain flavor.

Dill
A member of the parsley family with a distinctive flavor that is easily lost during heating. It can be used to flavor salads, vegetables, meats, and sauces. The seeds are most often used for the brine in which dill pickles are cured.

Fennel
Florence fennel is a perennial plant with foliage used in salads, stews, and soups and with a bulb cooked as a vegetable. Its flavor is similar to, but sweeter and more elusive than, anise. Common fennel is the variety from which seeds are harvested to use in both sweet and savory dishes.

Garlic
A member of the lily family and cousin to leeks, chives, onions, and shallots. Its highly aromatic flavor is used in most of the cuisines of the world, and it is reputed to have medicinal value as well. Pressing releases more of its essential oils than slicing.

Marjoram
A member of the mint family with a sweet flavor reminiscent of thyme and oregano, a strong aroma, and a cool aftertaste. It is used to flavor lamb, veal, and vegetables.

Mint
An aromatic family of herbs with over 30 species. It is used in both savory and sweet dishes, beverages, and as a garnish. Some of the species have flavors reminiscent of fruits, such as lemon, or other flavorings, such as chocolate.

Oregano
A member of the mint family, also known as wild marjoram, with a pungent, peppery flavor, used principally in Italian, Greek, and Mexican cuisines. It is especially good in dishes with a tomato foundation and in combination with basil.

Parsley
A mild herb with a slightly peppery, tangy flavor. Flat-leaf parsley is more strongly flavored than the curly-leaf variety. It is widely used as a flavor enhancer or garnish, but several cuisines base entire dishes on parsley as the main ingredient.

Rosemary
A member of the mint family with a strong flavor reminiscent of lemon and pine and a strong, sharp, camphorlike aroma. Originally used to cure ailments of the nervous system, it is used as a seasoning for fruit salads, soups, poultry, lamb, fish, and egg dishes.

Sage
Native to the Mediterranean, with a slightly bitter, musty, mint flavor, and used for both medicinal and culinary purposes. It is commonly used in dishes containing pork, cheese, or beans, and in poultry and game stuffings.

Savory
A relative of the mint family with a flavor and aroma reminiscent of a cross between thyme and mint. Winter savory has a more bitter and pungent flavor, also reminiscent of rosemary. It is used in pâtés, soups, meat, fish, and bean dishes.

Tarragon
An aromatic herb with a strong aroma and an assertive flavor reminiscent of anise with undertones of sage. It is widely used in classic French cuisine for chicken, fish, vegetables, and sauces. It is also an integral ingredient in fines herbes.

Thyme
A member of the mint family with a strong, slightly lemony flavor and aroma. It is widely used to flavor vegetables, meat, poultry, fish, soups, and cream sauces. It is basic to French cuisine and integral to bouquet garni.

High Altitude Baking

The higher the altitude, the less air pressure there is, a condition sometimes referred to as "thin air." The significance for cooking is that baked goods rise differently than at sea level and recipes need to be adjusted to accommodate that fact.

As a general rule, it helps to increase the baking temperature by 25 degrees. Reduce the baking powder using the list below, but don't reduce the baking soda by more than 1/2 teaspoon for each cup of acid liquid used. Also, grease baking pans well and dust with flour or line with waxed paper, because cakes have a tendency to stick at high altitudes.

In baking fruitcakes, omit the leavening completely. For angel food and sponge cakes, underbeat the eggs slightly or keep the eggs cold until ready to use to reduce the volume. Layer cakes are generally better textured at high altitudes than loaf cakes.

Yeast doughs also rise faster and higher at high altitudes. At 5,000 feet, use less yeast and shorten rising time to compensate for the weaker structure of the dough.

At 3,000 to 5,000 feet:
> Increase liquid by 1 to 2 tablespoons per cup.
> Decrease baking powder 1/8 teaspoon for every teaspoon.
> Increase baking temperature by 25 degrees.

At 5,000 to 7,000 feet:
> Increase liquid by 2 to 3 tablespoons per cup.
> Decrease baking powder by 1/8 to 1/4 teaspoon for every teaspoon.
> Decrease sugar 1 to 2 tablespoons per cup.
> Increase baking temperature by 25 degrees.

At 7,000 to 10,000 feet:
> Increase liquid by 3 to 4 tablespoons per cup.
> Decrease baking powder by 1/4 to 1/2 teaspoon for every teaspoon.
> Decrease sugar 2 to 3 tablespoons per cup.
> Increase baking temperature by 25 degrees.

Over 10,000 feet:
> Follow instructions for 7,000 to 10,000 feet.
> Add an extra egg, but do not overbeat the eggs.

Metric Conversions

Volume

These metric measures are approximate benchmarks for purposes of home food preparation.
1 milliliter = 1 cubic centimeter = 1 gram

Liquid	Dry
1 teaspoon = 5 milliliters	1 quart = 1 liter
1 tablespoon = 15 milliliters	1 ounce = 30 grams
1 fluid ounce = 30 milliliters	1 pound = 450 grams
1 cup = 250 milliliters	2.2 pounds = 1 kilogram
1 pint = 500 milliliters	

Weight

1 ounce = 28 grams
1 pound = 450 grams

Length

1 inch = $2^1/_2$ centimeters
$^1/_{16}$ inch = 1 millimeter

Formulas Using Conversion Factors

Use these formulas to convert measures from one system to another.

Measurements	Formulas
ounces to grams:	# ounces x 28.3 = # grams
grams to ounces:	# grams x 0.035 = # ounces
pounds to grams:	# pounds x 453.6 = # grams
pounds to kilograms:	# pounds x 0.45 = # kilograms
ounces to milliliters:	# ounces x 30 = # milliliters
cups to liters:	# cups x 0.24 = # liters
inches to centimeters:	# inches x 2.54 = # centimeters
centimeters to inches:	# centimeters x 0.39 = # inches

Approximate Weight to Volume

flour, all-purpose, unsifted	1 pound = 450 grams = $3^1/_2$ cups
flour, all-purpose, sifted	1 pound = 450 grams = 4 cups
sugar, granulated	1 pound = 450 grams = 2 cups
sugar, brown, packed	1 pound = 450 grams = $2^1/_4$ cups
sugar, confectioners'	1 pound = 450 grams = 4 cups
sugar, confectioners', sifted	1 pound = 450 grams = $4^1/_2$ cups
butter	1 pound = 450 grams = 2 cups

Temperature

Centigrade degrees x $^9/_5$ + 32 = Fahrenheit degrees; Fahrenheit degrees - 32 x $^5/_9$ = Centigrade degrees

Temperature	Fahrenheit	Centigrade
baking temperature	350°	177°
baking temperature	375°	190.5°
baking temperature	400°	204.4°
baking temperature	425°	218.3°
baking temperature	450°	232°

Acknowledgments

Professional Contributors

Tim Buckingham, Buck's Grill House, Moab
Tony Caputo, Tony Caputo's Market & Deli, Salt Lake City
Steve and Jenny Erickson, Ranui Gardens, Coalville
Trey Foshee, Sundance Foundry Grill, Provo Canyon
Jerry Garcia, Chez Betty, Park City
Terry Gross, Salt Lake City
Marguerite Henderson, Cucina, Salt Lake City
Joe Jennings and Randall Richards, Bit N Spur, Springdale
David Jones, Log Haven, Mill Creek Canyon, Salt Lake City
Adam Killpack, Slick Rock Cafe, Moab
Vicky Martinez, Beverage Director and Wine Buyer, Snowbird Ski & Summer Resort
Bill Oblock, Grapevine Restaurant, Logan
Gary Pankow, Café Diablo, Torrey
Upton Ramsey, Salt Lake City
Jane Sleight, Pack Creek Ranch, Moab
Liz Sprackland, Sundance Farms, Charleston
Mark Stamler, Food and Beverage Director, Snowbird Ski & Summer Resort
Victoria Topham, Pinon Market & Cafe, Salt Lake City
Mikel Trapp, Food and Beverage Director, Stein Erikson Lodge, Deer Valley

Contributors

Pat Adams	Jerry Brecke	Sue Conner	Carol Firmage
Suzanne Adams	Edie Brothman	Karen Cook	Karin Fojtik
Judy Aker	Ann Brown	Elizabeth Corso	Jennifer Foote
Scott Albert	Teresa Bruce	Alyce Covey	Tim Formosa
Katy Andrews	Karen Brunfleck	Melanie Cowley	Allene Fowler
Emily Ayre	Sally Burbidge	Dee Ann Cox	Janet Frasier
Perri Babalis	Fran Byrne	Karen Crockett	Patrick Frasier
Julie Baker	Terry Cagen	Christina Davis	Jacque Frei
Anne Barnes	Laurie Call	Debra Day	Chris Freymuller
Adrian Barrett	Marianne Campbell	Patrice Deane	Suzanne Frisch
Kimberly Barsketis	Gertrude Carlson	Nancy Dedman	Amy B. Funderburk
Cheri Beck	Catherine D. Carroll	Barbara Denton	Fiona Garda
Caryn Beck-Dudley	Caroline Carter	Carole Dixon	Keri Gardner
Krista Benedetti	Chris Casper	Allison Dorius	Janice Gaskill
Maureen Bennett	Carolyn Castelman	Lynn Dudley	Catherine Gentry
Vicki Bennett	Janine Cathcart	Shae Dudley	Mary Gilchrist
Tricia Bennion	Ruth Catron	Sheri Dunleavy	Melanie Gilstrap
Vicki Bennion	Ruben Ceballos	Brooke Dyer	Jan Glass
Corinne Bergmann	Lori Chambers	Vickie Echternucht	Chris Graves
Igor Best-Devereux	Liz Classen	Elaine Ellertson	Cyndi Graves
Lenka Best-Devereux	Beverly Cleghorn	Kimberly Ellis	Tierney Groy
Shauna Bollinger	Jane Ann Coats	Mary Lynne Erickson	Joan Hammarstrom
Shannon Bond	Julia Collard	Cathi Erlandson	Carolyn Hansen
Carol Brandi	Kelly Colopy	Denise Farnes	Eileen Hansen
Mary K. Brandi	Barbara Conner	Sherry Feldman	Peggy Hansen
Jennifer Brassey	Cynthia Conner	LeAnne Fine	Mia Harris

Cathy Hartman
June Hartman
Sally Heim
Tricia Heinz
Holly Henriod
Lorraine Henriod
Shelley Henriod
Rise Hirabayashi
Susan Hollberg
Nancy Holman
Maribeth Howard
Judy Huber
John Hudson
Rebecca Hyde
Heidi Ingham
Marian Ingham
Marion Inman
Jennifer Jackson
Mary Jarrell
Cheryl Johnson
Linda Johnson
Agnes Jones
Dena Jones
Stephanie Juhl
Josie Jukes
Liz Kaminsky
Jennifer Kelsey
Teresa Kemp
Josie Kimball
Linda Kimmel
Naomi Schweitzer
    King
Anne Kirkpatrick
Sandra Klade
Gene Klatt
Pat Klein
Layle Koncar
Rose Koskimaki
Dorothy Kraus
Greg Kraus
Carol Kroesche
Anna Lee Kuhr
Joanne Kuwada
Rholinda Lange
Evelyne Lanvers
Diana Lapage
Jackie Lassen
Margaret Latey
Terri LaTourette
Pat Lauer
Devin Layman

Allison Leishman
Alison Lesieutre
Sherlyn Lewis
Suzanne Ley
Liz Lockette
Julie Lund
Cindy Lundgren
Lisa Lyall
Cynthia Lyman
Sharlene Lyons
Susan Macfarlane
Tami Macfarlane
Noelle Madsen
Crystal Magellet
Heidi Makowski
Rosanne Marquardson
Carol Marriott
Jeff Martinez
Monica Martinez
Susan Massey
Susan Matte
Judy Matthews
Patricia Mattson
Kimberly McDermett
Simone McInnis
Lisa Hale McMillan
Jane McQuade
Susie Meier
Lisa Mietchen
Kathie Miller
Emily Monroe
Toni Montrone
David Moore
Shirley Moore
Suzanne Pierce Moore
Laura Moseley
Jean Munk
Monica Myrick
Jennifer Nash
Barbara Nelson
Deanne Nelson
DeEtte Nelson
Leigh Neumayer
Jonn Nishiyama
Blair Norman
Betty Oberman
Wendy Ogden-
    Crawley
Lisa Olsen
Nanette Olsen
Sandra Olsen

Joanie Packard
Jane Pankow
Pam Pannier
Tiffany Parker
Kathy Pederson
Cathy Pellicani
Anne Pendo
Diana Perog
Kristine Perog
Helen Peters
Victoria Peters
R. J. Peterson
Sandra Peterson
Sandy Peterson
Pam Phillips
Cheryl Pitkin
Janice Poulson
Mary Pusey
Jana Quilter
Virginia Rainey
Mary Rasmussen
Barbara Reese
Sharon Reichel
Susan Reid
Josephine Reynolds
Elizabeth Richter
Debbie Ritter
Jeane Robinson
Carolyn Roll
Jennifer Rose
Charlene Roth
Kim Ruud
Janette Sakellariou
Margaret Sargent
Chris Schmitt
Kay Schultz
Duchess Schuman
Joe Scully
Brenda Shockey
Olga Siggins
Anne Sill
Lynda Simmons
Carla Smith
Nancy Smith
Shannon E. Smith
Chris Snieckus
Nancy Souder
Therese Stangl
Cindy Steenblik
Ronda Landa Steinau
Teresa Stepanek

Vallee Stetner
Joanne Stevenson
Kellie Stevenson
Mary Stoneman
Karen Strasser
Maggie Strasser
Connie Sturzenegger
Angela Sudbury
Alison Swillinger
Kerry Riordan Sykes
Kathy Taiclet
Rosemary Tepper
Jan Thorpe
Joanne Trealoff
Janet Underwood
Polly Unruh
Allison Van Vranken
Stephanie Veasy
Julie Verdecchia
Holly Virden
Lori Wadsworth
Aleesa Walthers
Scott Wangsgard
Susan Warner
Julia Watkins
Cindi Watko
Marilyn Watts
Bonnie Weiss
Paulette Welch
Lynette Weller
Teri Weller
Judy White
Marcia White
Melany White
Abbie Whitney
Debi Williams
JoAnn Williams
Jane Wise
Cali Wolf
Laura Wolf
Angie Woltjen
Bob Wood
Kellie Wood
Stephanie Woodland
Gwen Wright
Anna Yates
Alice Young
Amy Young
Nancy Young

Index

220

Always in Season

A Collection of Recipes from the
Junior League of Salt Lake City, Utah
438 East 200 South, Suite 200
Salt Lake City, Utah 84111
(801) 328-4516

Please send me _____ copies of *Always in Season* $21.95 each $ _____

Postage and handling for first book to each address $ 4.00 each $ _____

Additional books shipped to the same address $ 1.00 each $ _____

Total $ _____

Name

Street Address

City   State   Zip

Telephone Number

[   ] VISA   [   ] MasterCard

[   ] Check enclosed made payable to the Junior League of Salt Lake City

Account Number   Expiration Date

Cardholder Name

Signature

Photocopies will be accepted.